Being with Becky

LISA BINKOWSKI

ARPress

ARPress
45 Dan Road Suite 5
Canton MA 02021
Hotline: 1(888) 821-0229
Fax: 1(508) 545-7580

Ordering Information:
Quantity sales. Special discounts are available on quantity purchases by corporations, associations, and others. For details, contact the publisher at the address above.

Printed in the United States of America.

ISBN-13:   Softcover   979-8-89389-651-0
                  eBook   979-8-89389-652-7

Library of Congress Control Number: 2024921472

PREFACE

I wrote *BEING WITH BECKY* to honor my sister Rebecca, recollecting special times we shared throughout the course of her life. When she died, I spent a lot of time writing my thoughts and feelings about her absence. In between each chapter of our experiences, I've inserted these thoughts; hence, "thoughts in between." All of these thoughts and all of the chapters of our times are purely from my point of view and not intended to take away from anyone else's experiences with her. I have written about what I know to be my truths and the facts as I understand them.

I want to thank the following individuals who helped shape these experiences: my Mom and Dad, Rick, Danita, Sara, Steve, John, Mary, Joe, Richard, and Marsha. A special thanks goes to Caroline and Sue for their assistance in getting this book completed. Finally, my deepest gratitude goes to Becky for all the laughter, warmth, compassion and love. My intent is to share her story, not just because she died, but because of how she lived. Her life is a story worth repeating.

CHAPTER 1

Remembering Rebecca

Have you ever experienced the unexpected loss of someone very close to you in a way you never imagined or even remotely considered? Well, I have. It's the most devastating, horrifying, painful thing a person can endure. I would suspect many people who've had such an experience never really manage to actually *endure* it and the unbearable aftermath. It's so easy to sadly disappear inwardly and continue an existence in an empty shell, surviving only because of human nature's instinct for survival. The loss can feel so consuming that one might not want to go on, let alone enjoy the journey ahead. How can anyone expect a survivor to go on? Or even more difficult, how can someone enjoy the journey of going on?

Unfortunately, I understand how hard it is to be a survivor. When Becky died, I wanted to die right there with her. No, I wanted to die instead of her. I wanted to be the one to go. But, of course, we don't get to make those choices; we are left behind to live. When Becky died, my life was shattered into millions of pieces, and I have never been the same. After her death, I spent so much time picking up the pieces of myself, trying to figure out who I was and what I was supposed to do with my life, and grappling with the question of why I was still here that I was barely alive.

All these years later I still don't have all the answers I desperately hope to find. I think about Becky all the time and think If you knew her, you would probably think of her quite often, too. And, if you never had the privilege of sharing any part of life with her, then I think you would want to get to know her. She would prefer you call her Rebecca, but to me, she'll always be Becky.

THOUGHTS IN BETWEEN NUMBER 1

Pretty Hair long
    curly
      short
        straight
          sun-lightened blonde
            always changing the style of her hair

Beautiful Woman
    beautiful eyes
      beautiful smile
        perfect body
          toned
            full
              sleek
                voluptuous
                  strong
                    never satisfied with it

Beautiful Soul
 dreamer
  doer
   warm
    caring
     spirited
      determined
       loyal
        a loving heart for everyone

Beautiful You
 sister
  friend
   housemate
    companion
     Tallulah
      Becky
       Rebecca

CHAPTER 2

Introduction

The date was February 25, 1993, and although winters are always challenging in Northwest Ohio, this day was particularly brutal. The temperature hovered in the single digits, and the winds blustered along from fifteen to twenty miles an hour. Snow had fallen the past several days, and it coated the ground four to six inches deep. As I drove through the cemetery gates off Parkside Boulevard, I looked around to the place where we would gather one more time to be with her.

As I pulled the car to a halt with Marsha sitting beside me, other cars followed close behind. I climbed out of the car and tugged desperately on my scarf to ward off the cold, but to no avail. One by one, the others climbed out of their vehicles and braced themselves for the bitter chill. The wind ripped through our bundles of coverings as if to mock our futile attempt to stay warm. No one said a word as we stared ahead to the area resting under the large crucifix. This is where we would say goodbye to her for the last time.

My brother-in-law George reached into the trunk and pulled out a metal folding table and carried it towards the cross, as Danita, my sister, tucked a large candle under her arm and walked with him. Two of their three daughters followed behind. Caitlin, the oldest at seven, marched behind, carefully stepping in her Dad's footsteps, while Hanna, who had recently turned six, grabbed Marsha's hand as she shuffled through the snow. I reached into the back seat of my car and grabbed a small book, along with a cassette player, as my brothers, Rick, Steve, John and Joe joined me in the trek to the large cross. Another sister, Sara, with her husband Mark, slowly climbed out of their car and headed our way.

Walking slowly in the middle of our group was Richard, her fiancé, who drove in from Kalamazoo, in spite of the weather, to be with us today. Jeff, my brother John's good friend and family friend for years, had joined my brothers, and as he piled out of the vehicle, our mom stepped towards him and handed her video camera to him without saying a word. He nodded politely to her, understanding what she asked in the silence. Our sister Mary had gone back to her home in Orange, California, with her husband Scott a couple of weeks before. Mary was heartsick that she was unable to return to Toledo to be with us, and as difficult as this day was for all of us who were there, I felt badly for her that she couldn't stay and be with the family. My Dad was the last one out of the car, and he cautiously carried a plain metal container in his hands as he prodded through the snow towards the looming crucifix.

This particular area of Calvary Cemetery was designed for persons who were cremated. The Catholic Church forbade cremation for a long time; however, several years before 1993, the Church had lifted the ban on burials for cremated Catholics. Two sections of this cemetery were allocated for these kinds of burials, and a couple weeks before, we had met and decided as a family that Becky would appreciate this final resting place in the shadows of Jesus on His crucifix. She would always be there by His side, and we knew that this would be what she would have wanted.

There were actually three sides to the structure, with a crucifix mounted on dark marble pillars on each side, standing somewhere near twenty feet tall, surrounded by four steps on each side in an even triangle. Out from the steps were two rows of burial plots, some with inscriptions of previously deceased and others blank. Her plot was on the end, with the concrete cover lying off to the side of it, exposing an opening about six inches square just under the reaches of the outstretched arms of Jesus. He would watch over her from now on.

Out in front of the plots, George set his folding table up and steadied the legs against the wind and deep snow. Dani stood her pillar candle on the table and placed a glass cylinder around it to try to thwart off the wind. John pulled out his lighter and ignited the wick, something he did repeatedly while we were there. I put the cassette player on the end of the table and pushed the play button. A soft, somber melody began, and although it was meant to be soothing, the sounds were haunting. This was a tape found in her apartment when we gathered her things, a collection of songs she listened to while studying or taking time for a little peace and quiet. To me, these songs, this music, would always be a reminder of this day, and no matter how beautiful the melodies were, they were just one more sign that she was gone.

When I saw the small, square shaped hole cut into the ground about a foot deep and knew that's where Becky would be, I had to immediately force my brain to consider some other topic. I tried quickly to come up with any other thought besides what I knew would fit into that small opening, and then I saw the tin that my father carried to the grave. I started trembling, choking back the inevitable tears, gasping to catch my breath.

Dad set the tin on the table next to the candle, and by that time, as I looked around, everyone was crying. Everyone but my mother, whose face, despite the wind and cold was pale and still, as if she'd been put in a trance. Her emotions were frozen, not by the cold, but by this horrific loss, and I don't know if it was her sheer inner strength or the complete collapse of her ability to feel anything that dominated her being.

What I do know is that this loss changed each and every one of us in more ways than we could ever imagine, and simple things like satisfying hunger, or falling asleep when tired, were no longer simple. Sometimes, just breathing in and out was an effort. I looked around at my siblings and my parents and Richard and mumbled that we should get started.

"Who wants to go first? Anyone who wants to say anything, go ahead," I said quietly. Mom started talking about how Becky was not only her daughter, but her friend, her good friend, and how she misses her smile. She talked about her as a high schooler and how she could never spell well. She spoke of how she had such a wonderful way with people and had such a unique way of making each person feel special. Rick then said that although Becky was spoiled as the last child of this large family, Mom and Dad saved the best for last. Dani spoke eloquently of Becky's influence on not only our family but countless people she touched. She then read a message sent from Mary, who wrote a letter to her younger sister she called "*Peke*," a fond nickname she gave Becky for being her maid of honor at her wedding in Hawaii. I also wrote a letter to Becky that I read aloud as everyone stood weeping, huddled together.

"Dear Beck," I started. "I've seen your face a million times in the last twenty-three days. Has it been twenty-three days? It seems like yesterday when I got the call. Time seems to have stood still, and yet I know better. I want the world to stop, and yet, I want time to fly and to carry this pain away with it. How are we supposed to live the rest of our lives without you?" I asked through my tears. "How can we make it through the day on memories? The pain we feel is overwhelming, immeasurable, overbearing. What, my sweet little sister, can we do? I try really hard to believe that you're in a better place; I think that you are. I try to understand that God took you to share in His glory; I believe that you are there with Him. And I trust that the life you gave to this cruel and angry world will make a difference. The rest of my life depends upon it. Maybe you were too good for this human living, Becky, and God has given you a new life. I pray to you and implore the heavens to help us with your leaving. Life is ever changing; we all know that. In your death is a new beginning for all of us. Help us, Becky, to have the courage to survive this change and to live beyond this change, to trust and hope that God will gently guide us as we begin a new path without you. Help us, inspire us, and hold us in these most impossible times. I love you; I've loved you every day of your life. I promise I'll love you every day of mine. Hold my hand when you see me tremble. Hug me tight when I cry.

Know that I'll do my best to make you proud. And save me a spot near you for when it's my turn to go. I believe I'll see you again someday. And for that, I can't say goodbye. I'll just say see you later." And then I shared a short poem from *Wings of Silver*, a collection by Jo Petty of works by unknown authors:

The clock of life is wound but once,

And no man has the power to tell

Just when the hands will stop

At late or early hour.

Now is the only time you own;

Live, love, toil with a will,

Place no faith in tomorrow;

For the clock may then be still.

I needed to say something to Becky, about Becky, and for Becky. I didn't really know what else to do. Dad wiped tears away from his face as he picked up the tin and cradled it in his arms. His words were the culmination of this painful farewell.

"This is about what she weighed when she was born," he uttered through his sobs.

I just stared at the tin as he carefully placed it back on the table. I could not pick it up, even though in a strange way, I wanted to. I remember when she was a baby, and I could remember my Dad leaving for the hospital to take Mom to have this baby. To equate the contents of that tin with a newborn made me struggle for air. Why did this happen, I thought to myself.

I've asked the same question over and over and over, until I've been numb to the thought of anything else. And as I stood there in the bitter cold, I knew there would never be an answer to that question of *why*. I can only answer the question as to *what is*, and the fact is, we are burying her today, and nothing makes this truth more absolute. There are no more chances for remote miracles that there was some terrible mistake in identity or that any of us would awake from the nightmare and go back to life as it was. Our reality is that she was buried here today, and we'll never see her again. It's an excruciating truth, one that will haunt me the rest of my life.

THOUGHTS IN BETWEEN NUMBER 2

Often times I find myself staring out the window, hoping to catch a glimpse of her passing by. I know it's probably my imagination, but I swear there've been times that I've seen her, walking slowly, as if her feet barely touch the ground. Sometimes she's deep in the trees; other times she's right in the middle of traffic on a busy road. She's always wearing a long white, flowing kind of gown, and her hair bounces softly as if there's a gentle breeze blowing through. I stare silently as she reaches her arms out as she walks, sometimes inviting nearby wildlife, other times children gathering at her feet, always with a sweet innocent smile on her face. Sometimes she stops and turns her head to gaze in my direction. Chills run up and down my spine and I lose my breath as I find our eyes connecting. I want to run out to her and touch her, and kiss her cheek, and tell her how much I love her and miss her. But I'm frozen; I just stare and she slowly fades from my view.

Chapter 3

The Binkowski Family

I was thirteen years old when she was born into our family; the fifth girl, the ninth child. Certainly, she wasn't intended; our parents struggled to make ends meet raising nine children. My Dad, Stephen Stanley Binkowski, worked full time as a draftsman and managed a wedding photography business on the side. His experience taking pictures while in the Navy during the Korean War sparked his interest and helped him develop his skills in photography. He spent most of his weekends taking pictures for weddings. He was a pure craftsman from start to finish and cornered a part of the house into a darkroom where he developed and processed his own black and white prints. Once the industry began shifting over to color photography, he weaned himself from the professional business and indulged mostly in landscape and floral subjects as a hobby. He was always so good at his work in the wedding business, but when the escalating prices in color development forced his business prices to rise, he found it difficult to increase his prices enough to keep up with the market. Plus, he would have needed to invest in the color processing equipment, and with eleven mouths to feed, it just wasn't feasible.

During the early years when my father took those wedding pictures, he often used our living room as the site for the bridal portraits that would appear in the local newspaper. I can recall my Mother scurrying about, cleaning the house and then shuffling us off to another room so that we wouldn't disturb the interaction between my father and the bride to be. Sometimes we would peek out around the corner just to catch a glimpse, but usually it was my job to corral the younger siblings out of the way. I don't think any of us ever understood why we couldn't just sit and watch, but to my Dad, always the perfectionist, having gawking children around was absolutely unacceptable.

The wonderful thing about his passion for photography was that he took hundreds of pictures of his family throughout the years. He captured so many memories in our early years, and even as his interests leaned more toward flowers and scenery, his love of photography rubbed off on several of his kids, as well as on my mom. We bought her first camera for her on Mother's Day in 1983, and despite a lot of critiquing from my dad, she's been the one who has taken more pictures than anybody. My mom, Mary Ann Slowinski, is a woman never too shy to stand in front of or behind the camera, creating "moments" or trying to capture them on film or video. Between her, my dad, and many of my siblings, we have so many pictures of our family that it would take months to sift through them all. It seems each of us with a camera takes a shot of the same pose, and when we share them later, many pictures are the same. Still, each one is a treasure in itself, and I thank God for this love of picture taking, because it's one of the wonderful ways I've been able to hold on to Becky since she died.

My family is a pretty amazing collection of eleven individuals, but the most notable ingredient of the Binkowski clan has always been our incredible devotion to one another. My parents, the diligent providers that they were, struggled faithfully to make ends meet. And while my dad was working his two jobs and my mom worked her midnight job, we often relied on each other for company. Throughout the years, maybe because of this reliance, we have remained remarkably close. In some ways, we're a rather odd bunch, because we may spend an entire day together, say the longest goodbyes, and then talk about meeting for breakfast the next morning. It's always been rare for any of us to grow tired of each other. Sure, we've had countless squabbles; what family doesn't? But, for as long as I can remember, there has been an incredibly deep bond woven between each of us. It's not that our parents were ever overtly affectionate in front of us; on the contrary, actually. With all of the responsibilities of work and home and family, they had their hands full. I'm not quite sure what kind of magic filled our home as we grew up, but the love was real and the connection is amazingly strong. Even as my folks scraped by, we felt like we were blessed. I can remember every September we'd head to the nearest Picway Shoe Store, where my parents could purchase two pairs of school shoes for five dollars. We were always excited to go to Picway, maybe because we didn't know any better, but we were happy and grateful just the same.

Hand me down clothes seemed to work just fine for most of us, too. I can't begin to remember how many shirts and pants I'd worn from my older brother Rick. It was okay with me. Many times our evening meals would consist of macaroni and cheese, ten cent pot pies, or large cans of tomato soup with noodles. A very special treat every now and then was a short trip to the new McDonald's down on Cherry Street. We could each get a fifteen cent hamburger and then split a bag of small French fries with a brother or sister. Our family vacation consisted of traveling to Cedar Point, an amusement park about 60 miles east of Toledo. Of course, Mom and Dad packed sandwiches and containers of Kool- Aid for lunch, but every year we ate fried chicken at one of the park's restaurants. Sometimes, we were treated to a mid-day snack, although most of the time we were responsible for our own purchases with whatever money we had earned or saved from birthdays or the tooth fairy. We never got allowances for home chores because there wasn't any money to give. Besides, we had jobs to help the family, and that's what we did. We never had the opportunity for many extras growing up, but I don't ever remember feeling like we were missing out on anything. We each had our own friends, but living in such tight quarters and spending so much time together led us to befriend each other as well. I look back on my youth and I don't recall being jealous of other kids who had more things or took better vacations. What we had, and still do to this day, is an intangible wealth in our relationships with one another. They are truly incomparable, and for that, I will always be thankful.

THOUGHTS IN BETWEEN NUMBER 3

Life is a journey,
full of wonder, discovery, and excitement.

Life is a challenge,
full of disappointment, heartache and sorrow.

Life is a blessing,
full of joy, hope and love.

Life, in some ways, is exactly the same for each of us,
but in other ways, it is different, personal and unique.

What we take from life is that which is given so naturally—
the breadth and depth of being alive.

What we give to life is all a matter of choice.

CHAPTER 4

The Early Years

I can remember when she was born. There were already ten of us living in a small, one story home on Northgate Street in west Toledo. The house, about 900 square feet of living space, had three identical bedrooms, one small bath, and a modest living room. In 1967, when Becky was born, the four boys shared one bedroom, while the four girls shared another. There were two sets of bunk beds on either side of these two bedrooms, with a single dresser separating the two beds. With a baby coming into our home, Mom and Dad were forced to share their room with the newborn. They squeezed a crib at the rear of their bed, which was the only option available at the time. This arrangement lasted just a few months, and soon my folks were house hunting. Raising nine children was an enormous task, and I'm sure, quite challenging financially. It was difficult to find an affordable house with room for nine kids in which to grow. I can remember driving around on Sundays packed into the station wagon, traveling all over town looking for a new place to call home.

Eventually, Mom and Dad selected a house in Birckhead Place, a quaint neighborhood in the north part of Toledo, surrounded by a tall, spiked fence with a gated entrance. The neighborhood was developed in the early forties by several Polish American families attempting to fortress their culture and provide security during the challenging times of World War II. I recall those gates being closed only once in my years living there, but I suppose they were closed during the area's earlier days. With only 72 homes within the walls of Birckhead Place, it seemed a perfect place to raise a family. Outside travelers rarely passed through those gates, primarily because there is only one entrance and exit to the neighborhood, and mostly because the streets are made of bricks which have settled unevenly and created huge dips and bumps at every turn. Any driver attempting to speed more than five or six miles an hour in Birckhead would likely have regrets. Although tough on drivers, it was great for kids, because we never had to worry about speeding cars. It was pretty safe to run about freely and always fun to ride bikes on the bumpy streets.

And so, this little community was a cozy place to let kids run loose and make friends. There were lots of families like ours, not many as large, but lots of kids of all ages to play with. Plus, the Catholic high school was just around the block, and the Polish Catholic Church was within walking distance. Both were high on the list of considerations for our family's new home.

I don't remember exactly why or when, but at some point all of us kids started referring to our place of residence as simply "Birckhead." It sounds rather elitist to live in a gated community, but in reality, Birckhead was comprised of predominately large families, a handful of elderly couples, varied small sized families, and about a half dozen homes for the sisters and priests who taught at the high school. Nestled in-between the two blocks of houses were two large undeveloped pieces of land set aside as play areas. The front and back parks, as they were called, were great places to play football, whiffle ball, frisbee, or just take walks around the perimeter. It was a wonderful setting and a comfortable, friendly place to grow up.

In the early years of our living there, a group of adults who formed the Birckhead Board of Trustees planned annual parades for the Fourth of July, where we'd ride our decorated bikes through the streets, dressed in red, white and blue. Then we'd have a picnic, complete with games and prizes for the children. Every Fourth of July after the festivities were over, we'd go home and watch the six o'clock news to see if any of us made it on television for the parade coverage. And every Christmas season, we'd join some of the other neighbors and go caroling from house to house, singing at the top of our lungs until we were too cold to continue. We'd grab our song sheets and stop to entertain whoever would open their doors to listen for a song or two. Sometimes, they'd offer us hot chocolate to take off the chill. Those were great times in Birckhead! After settling into our new home, I know that things got tighter financially. Mom took a part-time job working nights as a switchboard operator at Flower Hospital just about a mile from Birckhead. Her shift was 11:00 pm to 7:00 am, and she often worked three nights a week. With only one car in the family, Dad would drive her to and from work. On school mornings, she would fix lunches, hustle most of us off to school, and take care of the younger kids until nap time. I know she rarely got the sleep she needed and spent the better part of the next four or five years tired. As I think now about my mom during those times, I'm amazed at her strength, and I know any inner strength I might have, I got from her.

Because Mom slept in the evenings before work and because raising nine children was a tremendous challenge, I was quite involved in taking care of Becky, Joey, and Mary, the three youngest kids. I kind of took over watching Becky most of the time, and we developed a special a fondness for each other very early in her life. There were times she called me "Mom" accidentally, which irked my Mother but touched me deeply. I adore all of my siblings, but there was always a unique bond between Becky and me. I think a lot of it had to do with the timing of her birth and my age when she was born. I was just getting old enough to be given some significant responsibilities, and caring for her was often my number one priority. I fed her, changed her, rocked her, and played with her as she grew. Although there were thirteen years between us, we were connected from the beginning.

At some point in those first years in Birckhead, Dad gave most of his children nicknames. There was no logical meaning behind any of them, and I think they were just an expression of his sense of humor. My nickname was "Ralph," Dani's was "George," and Sara's "Frank."

It was apparent that these nicknames were meant for private family kidding until Dad started calling Becky "Tallulah." Mom said he liked the actress, Tallulah Bankhead, and for no obvious reason, he gave that name to his youngest daughter. Dad often called her Tallulah throughout her life, and it was just one of those things that was weirdly sweet in the Binkowski home.

Unlike the rest of us, Becky embraced her nickname. It became so common that often times many of us in the family called her Taloo instead of Becky. When Becky was away at college, she even signed birthday cards and letters with Tallulah or Taloo.

I often think of the composition of my family and reflect on how each of us helped shape the entity of the "Binkowski's." Even though eleven individuals grew together in a single dwelling, in so many ways we are very different from one another. And then, in other ways, we are so much alike. My father, the meticulous photographer, was an exceptional artist as well. His specialty was oil painting, both portraits and landscapes. I had always heard that oil paints are one of the more difficult mediums to use, but that's what he preferred. He went through a period of a few years where he painted a variety of canvasses, and years later we were all given one of his paintings for Christmas. Several of my siblings have the same artistic ability as my father. My oldest brother Rick is extremely talented, both artistically and intellectually. Danita, or Dani, as we call her, two and a half years my junior, is much like Rick in both art and intelligence. So is John, the rebel child of the family. Steve, a year and a day older than John, always had a knack for drawing, too, although he didn't spend much time past his high school days pursuing art.

On the other side of the family coin, Mom lacked the gift of drawing and painting, but she played the piano and had a beautiful voice. I can remember when I was still in grade school, she'd tell me, "You're just like me; you can't draw a straight line." I always hoped that maybe I'd have opportunities to make music of some kind, whether playing an instrument or singing. When Rick was in the 8th grade, my folks arranged for him to take organ lessons, and he stayed with it for about a year. Being the genius that he was, he picked up the basics easily and from that point on, he learned to play not only the organ and the piano, but the guitar as well, on his own. I had asked to take lessons, too, but we couldn't afford the extra expense, and I had to wait my turn. I never did get a chance to take lessons, so when I was about 16 years old, I started teaching myself how to play the guitar on a cheap, old guitar I bought from a neighbor kid for ten dollars. I was a blooming folkie from then on.

In looking back to the musical genes of my mother, many of us were blessed with her love and gift of music. She used to sing around the house in a beautiful soprano voice—children's songs, TV theme shows, favorites from her own youth, or current songs on the radio. Music often filled the air in our home, and several of my siblings and I developed a passion for music in one way or another.

Rick, as I said, learned to play the organ, as well as the guitar and piano, and developed a skill to where he could figure out songs just by listening to them on the radio. I, of course, indulged in the guitar and enjoyed singing in the choir at church in grade school. My sister Sara, a year and a half younger than Danita, inherited the same beautiful voice as my mother, while John and Joey got wrapped up in rock and roll and playing electric guitar. Becky was in several musical shows in high school, and although she never had the lead part, she loved to sing and dance too.

In the early years of our family life, even before we moved to Birckhead, the British invasion was at its peak, and the Beatles were a common topic of conversation. Actually, more than conversation, as we often pretended to be the Beatles, blaring their tunes on a little box-like record player, mouthing the lyrics, and using household items as substitutes for instruments. Usually it was the four older kids fronting for the Fab Four, with Rick pretending to play the keyboard drawn on a cardboard box, Dani and I emulating clever guitar licks by strumming on tennis rackets, and Sara with a couple of pencils on top of a coffee can. We thought we were pretty darn good!

Although my father wasn't musically inclined, he always loved to listen to Polish music. Traditionally on Sunday mornings, Dad would tune in to his favorite Polka station on the radio, and with heavy accents, Chet and Helen would entertain us with hearty Polish songs. Many times we would dance around the living room, laughing giddily. Sometimes, even Mom and Dad would dance to a song or two, and the entire family would swing and sway to the lively Polish music. Becky seemed to get hooked on it early, too, and as she grew, she proudly sang along whenever the opportunity presented itself. Often, it was in church at St. Hedwig's in the heart of the Polish Village of North Toledo.

We were introduced to our Polish heritage very early in life. With the Binkowski and Slowinski marital union, we learned a variety of ethnic traditions that often coincided with holidays or other special events.

Dani, Sara, Mary and Becky grew fond of the traditions, and enjoyed the music they were taught in grade school. I was always passionate about several of the customs, but not really the music itself. I suppose that's because when we moved to Birckhead, I had just finished eighth grade and was headed to the Catholic high school. Dani and the rest of the kids went to St. Hedwig's grade school, where the music, customs and traditions were routinely conveyed to the students. Rick and I missed out on that, and I don't think Rick really cared about it anyway. I didn't realize what I had missed until I was much older.

As a tight knit Catholic family, we were all expected to attend mass every Sunday. Although my father didn't often attend with us, he never allowed us to skip the service. And so, Mom would pack everyone into the family station wagon and haul us off to church. People there would often stare at our entourage as we often arrived late. I don't think they necessarily stared because we were late, but because we were impossible to miss. Over time, everyone got to know the "Binkies," as we were often called collectively. Nine "towheads," as people often referred to blonde haired children, every one of us smaller than average, most often obedient and respectful, and always sticking together—those were the Binkowski children. As Rick closed in on his high school years, he fought the push to attend church, which I think a lot of teens, especially boys did in those rebellious periods. My other brothers probably reacted much the same way, but by their teenage days I was already out of college and living on my own. I would suspect my sisters were much like me, not always eager to attend mass, but like the dutiful daughters, most often attempting to do the right thing.

As a kid growing up in a deeply rooted Catholic family, developing your own "faith" was always stressed as an important quest. I think that it's more than just a constant belief in God, that perhaps it's more a way of living than anything else. I guess I see it as an unwavering sense of knowing that there is perpetual goodness in all living things. Bad things happen, but with faith, goodness will prevail, some way, somehow. The source of this faith may very well be in God, as the source of all goodness, as we were taught in Catholic schools. Or, perhaps, it is a belief in a different kind of spiritual entity, not rooted in any religious dogma. Whatever it is or however one may define it, anyone who knew Becky knew that she had an incredible faith.

Even as a young girl of five or six years old, she had a remarkable spirit and a tender but insightful sense of faith. She was passionate about life and the people and things that filled her world. I can recall her in church, singing at the top of her lungs, her joyful spirit resonating in the air. At home, playing with Joey or Mary, her laughter was infectious. And during the times when my father exercised his discipline with a stern hand, Becky stood by the ones getting questioned or punished. She carried this unwavering sense of faith throughout all of her life. It's just one of the many things about her that I continue to admire and appreciate.

My father used some rather serious methods of disciplining us, and by today's standards, would border on the edge of abuse. Getting spanked with a leather belt was the customary means of punishment, and I remember too many whacks across my bottom for errors of my youth. I know my brothers received more slaps with that belt than I would dare to count, but I don't think my dad ever hit Becky with it. Even the times when he would expect one of us to come forward and sheepishly announce who was guilty of leaving the lights on or not putting the toys away, he would punish all of us if no one stepped forward, but she never got the belt. Maybe he thought she was too young. Maybe he just thought she didn't deserve it. Regardless, she never suffered the wrath of my father's discipline like the rest of us. She was lucky. I think because of that, Becky developed a strong bond with my dad and never seemed to respond to his discipline as fearfully as the rest of us did. As she aged, she would challenge his actions she didn't approve of and questioned him without hesitation when he didn't agree with her perspectives. I always thought her responses were so bold and many times I envied them. She, on the other hand, often chided me for not being forthright in the same kind of situations. I always backed off and instead, suggested she talk to him because it seemed no one else could. As jealous as I may have gotten at times, I still marveled at her will to be honest and righteous. That kid had a lot of nerve, but in such a good way.

Thoughts in Between number 4

Being the youngest of nine children, Becky learned early on the importance of giving and sharing, the need for tolerance and patience, and the value of truthfulness and self-respect. As a young girl, she developed a stubbornness in defending the principles she believed essential to living a good Christian life. She carried this determination with her throughout her life's experience. Her unwillingness to compromise what she believed in became a trademark and a standard for others to follow when in her company.

In addition to her zest for righteous living, Becky developed a charm that could be both entertaining and inspirational. As the baby of the family, she knew quite well the ways to win someone's heart or to get her point across. But her intentions were never deceitful, and as easy as it could have been, she never indulged in manipulative acts to get her way. She had an innocence about her that complemented her charm and drew people to her. There was always something about Becky that made even strangers feel at home in her presence.

Chapter 5

Off To College

I left home for college at seventeen when Becky was four and a half. Mom said that she was upset that I was no longer around, even though I just went forty miles from home to Siena Heights College in Adrian, Michigan. I didn't have a driver's license, let alone a car, so my visits home were infrequent. Every now and then I would get a letter from Becky, dictated to Mary, who put the message on paper.

"Dear Lisa, I miss you. I hope you will come home . . . I wrote this letter by myself . . . I love, love you . . . write me a letter . . . ." Or, after her sixth birthday, she wrote, "Dear Lisa, how are you? I love you. Thank you for the card. I love you so much. Thank you for the kite . . . . . I have a lot to talk about Love and kisses, Becky."

Becky loved when a couple of friends would travel to Toledo to bring me home, and they would spend the evening with me and the family. During my sophomore year, I became close friends with a girl named Sandy, who went by the nickname "Sam." Sam was from Temperance, Michigan, just over the border, about twenty minutes from Birckhead.

Sam got to know Becky, and she adored her. The feeling was mutual. For some reason, they connected from the very beginning, and Becky wrote once to "tell Sam I love her." Sam and I used to play the guitar together, strumming John Denver songs over and over. Being the introvert that I was, I often let Sam do the singing while I played along. When I traveled home on my own, I played and sang to Becky, sometimes to Mary and Joey, too. Becky would sit and listen to so many John Denver tunes that she knew all the lyrics and chimed in when I would sing to her. She carried her fondness for his music throughout her life.

One of my favorites was a song called, *For Baby.* The lyrics were perfect from me to her: "I'll walk in the rain by your side; I'll cling to the warmth of your tiny hand; I'll do anything to keep you satisfied, and I'll love you more than anybody can. I'll be there when you're feeling down; to kiss away the tears when you cry; I'll share with you all the happiness I found; a reflection of the love in your eyes."

It always amazed me how much Becky enjoyed these times together. She could have been playing with her dolls or some other toy, but she regularly opted to sit with me while I played. I often look back at those times and just sit and enjoy the memories. Those times were priceless to me.

For her sixth birthday, my friend Sam made a special gift for Becky. On a large, rustic piece of driftwood she found along the shores of Lake Huron, she etched a message to her little friend: "Lying asleep in my arms, so tiny and soft, who can explore your secrets or see where you're going or discover where you've been? Though your life has just begun, you will grow beautiful, happy and free . . . For it is within your power to fly against sunsets, and master the four winds, to dare to be yourself, and cause others to do the same . . . be gentle, my baby; never losing your childlike manners; your innocence and gentleness is a lasting gift to those who love you "

I suppose I could have been jealous of such a beautiful gift for my sweet sister, but I was so taken aback by the impression that she had made on my 19 year old friend. This is what she did with her simple innocence and charming demeanor time and time again, to people who came in and out of her life. To the adults in Birckhead and others from the church, or college friends, Becky made an impact in ways that have always been hard to describe. I guess there are individuals like that, who seem to have a sense of purpose about them no matter what they do or where they go. To me, she was my youngest sister who loved hanging out with me and listening to me sing. Thirteen years between us may have influenced our interests and the nature of our interactions, but the bond in our hearts had no barriers.

Little did I know then how she could affect so many people just by being Becky.

Thoughts in between number 5

What will I do without you?

I'm missing you as a sister and as a friend. I'm missing the fun we used to have. I'm missing the talks we shared: you telling me about school, asking for advice about your boyfriend.

I miss spending time with you, laughing at silly things, going off on short adventures, practicing new dance moves with you.

What *will* I do without you?

What will our family do without you?

Family gatherings can never be the same. It's so hard to get together without you there. Do you know how hard it is to have family dinners, family pictures taken, even Rick and Jan's wedding, without you here? As hard as we try, it will never feel all right to be together without you.

What *will* our family do without you?

What will your boyfriend and friends do without you?

Best friends, companions, maybe soul mates, are now lost and alone. The closeness, the camaraderie, and the joy of your company have been taken and in their place, pain and loneliness have taken over.

What *will* they do without you?

What will the communities do without you?

The numerous children you cared for, the disabled, the underprivileged, and the ill, all kinds of people you gave to so eagerly and selflessly; what will they do without you?

Where is this God that you loved so much?

This all powerful, all giving, all knowing and all loving God; where is He, Beck? Please tell Him to teach us all how it can be possible to live without you because I think He is the only one who might know the answer. Until He unveils this mystery, living without you, at least for me, is next to impossible.

Chapter 6

Family Games

Our family thrived on games; ever since I was a young teenager, we played games for entertainment. With so many children to keep occupied and involved, my Mom and Dad would get us a different game each Christmas. Early favorites were *Family Feud* and Charades, where we would split into two teams and face off in answering questions. Usually, it was the girls against the boys, and from what I can remember, the girls won most of the time. I'm sure my brothers would dispute the claim, but their memories are likely not any better than mine these days. Anyway, we enjoyed the playful competition, sitting around the table, bantering in between questions and answers. I don't know if we ever completed a game in an expected time frame, because there was so much going on in addition to the game itself. In the mix of perfectionists, procrastinators, and analytical thinkers, there would be questions raised about the questions; questions raised about the answers given; questions raised about the length of time it took to answer the questions. We could make a simple game last hours, not intentionally, but because of the personalities of the players.

Once, when Becky was about 9 years old, we all sat down to play Charades. As usual, the girls faced off against the boys; even Mom and Dad joined in the fun. To play charades, each team wrote down titles of movies, TV shows, songs or books, folded the pieces of paper and put them in a bowl. A member of the opposite team pulled a paper out and was required to act out the title written on the paper, using no words or pointing to any clues. Their teammates had to guess the correct title in a specified amount of time. The game had been going along just fine when my brothers were stumped by the title of a book they could not guess. After time expired, my brother Steve announced the book's name:

"*Hello God, It's Me, Margaret,*" he explained in disappointment.

"What the hell kind of book is that?" My brother Rick yelled out angrily.

Right away Becky said, "It's a book I read in school."

"You mean you never heard of it, Rick?" My sister Dani asked teasingly.

The jesting didn't change Rick's mood; in fact, he got angrier at the comment. Pretty soon, all the boys in our house were complaining about the choice of book titles that ended up in our bowl.

"You should at least put the names of things that someone else would know," Steve exclaimed.

"You mean you never actually heard of this book? It's a very popular book for kids," Dani defended.

As the verbal battle continued, tempers flared. Finally, Rick got up from the couch and stomped over to get his coat out of the closet. As he put it on and prepared to leave, we all realized this had gone way too far.

"Come on Rick," I pleaded with him.

But I knew it was too late. He turned and walked out without saying good bye. Of course, all of us girls looked at each other and we knew we had won again. Trying hard to hide our delight, we agreed with the others that we would screen the titles next time. But, that was the last time we played charades as a family.

THOUGHTS IN BETWEEN NUMBER 6

Last night I begged the clock to stand still. I couldn't bear the thought of the day to come. I drank too much, I stared too long. Occasionally tears would quietly puddle in my eyes. I caught them with my sleeve before they made their way to my pillow and an obvious statement of where my heart had drifted off to. I fought sleep even as I lay in my tempting warm bed. But, hard as I tried, the day had found me. And I am drenched in memory of your death. And now, there is no escape from the truth. I have not seen you since this day, so long ago. And God, I miss you so damn much.

CHAPTER 7

Becky's Friendships

I don't think I've ever known anyone who has had as many friendships as Becky. From the time she was a small girl, she attracted people to her like a magnet. She was warm, kind, innocent, and fun. As a young girl, she had some good friends in the neighborhood, most especially her friend Marilyn, who lived just three doors down from us in Birckhead. Becky and Marilyn spent time together after school, on the weekends, and even moved in together when they got out of high school. I used to babysit Marilyn and her siblings, and Becky often went with me to hang out with Marilyn.

They had a genuine friendship that lasted her lifetime.

Becky also had a good friend Melanie, whom she met in high school. They hung out together as they got older, heading out to clubs and dances for nights out. Melanie was a trained dancer, and she taught Becky the latest dance moves to use on their evening outings. Sometimes their relationship was like fire and ice, but they had an incredible bond nonetheless. Becky and Melanie lived together for a short time, but they'd decided it was better to save their friendship and live apart rather than drive each other crazy. When Becky moved out of Melanie's apartment, she moved in with Dani and George at their house on Bancroft. Becky saved her friendship with Melanie and it was tight from then on.

Becky was friends with many different kinds of people. She had lots of male friends, which seemed a bit unusual, but was obviously totally natural for her. I think secretly every guy who befriended her fell in love with her a little bit. When she didn't pursue something more serious with them, they decided a friendship with Becky was better than no relationship with her. And so, she had lots of male friends. She was great at judging character; all of the young men she met and established friendships with were all good guys. If they weren't when they were away from her, then she brought out the best of them when they were with her. I think she did that with all of the people she spent time with. She had a way of drawing people towards her and making them feel special. When she made you feel special, she made you want to be the best person you could be. That's the effect she had on people, regardless of age, gender or class. Becky made us all want to be like her: caring, genuine, and good.

THOUGHTS IN BETWEEN NUMBER 7

Time: it flies by so quickly and yet, it often stands still. How can it do both at the same time? The years have gone by, and I don't need to look at the calendar to know that this is my truth. Lines have etched their way into my face and hands. The weariness has taken its toll in my heart. I have aged a thousand days and each has left its mark. I am no longer young, that's for sure, and I am no longer youthful, as I was always so glad to be.

You, on the other hand, remain beautiful and young, with a youthful spirit beaming in those lovely eyes.

You will always be the same, and sometimes that's really good to know, but other times, it's bitingly painful.

CHAPTER 8

Becky And Mom

There was a period of time when Becky and I were not as close as we were for the rest of our years together. Her mid teenage years were a time, like they were for just about every other teenager, of independence, invincibility, and some degree of rebellion. Although it's hard to remember her as a rebellious type, she had her moments. It seemed that she had mom wrapped around her finger, and she got her way most of the time. I recall the rest of us watching her behavior, usually with jealousy or frustration, because whenever she requested something from my mother, whether it was a plea for money or a desire to be taken somewhere (the mall, a friend's house, a dance, a party, etc.), mom always caved in and catered to Becky.

My mother also used to proofread Becky's homework and written projects for school. It seemed to me that as a student I was directed to the encyclopedia or the dictionary for proper spelling or statistical information. Becky, instead, went to Mom, and Mom would spend her time correcting papers and filling in the blanks. I often thought Becky's grades improved noticeably as Mom assisted with the school tasks. It wasn't fair, and I know I believed Becky was spoiled, mostly by my mother. I don't know if it was her charm or her innocence, or just the fact that she was the baby of the family, but this girl got her way with both of my parents. Although I hadn't lived at home in several years, by the time Becky was in sixth or seventh grade, I had heard the stories from my other brothers and sisters, especially Joey and Mary.

As I look back, I don't think that 13 years between two people's ages is more noticeable than when I was in my late 20's and Becky was the ripe age of 15. When I was a kid her age, we were poor; we had one car and a houseful of little people. She had it easy, and she had a wonderful relationship with my mom. Who wouldn't be jealous? When I was young, Mom picked on me for every imaginable behavior flaw she thought she saw in me. She sent me to charm school because I was a tomboy. She told me I was just like her, someone who couldn't even draw a straight line, even though there was an abundance of artistic ability running in our family genes. And, she even counted the number of times I would chew my food at the family dinners, because she thought I ate too slowly. And here was Rebecca, a girl who could do no wrong. I found it tough to take sometimes.

Still, Becky was my sister, and I adored her, even if I didn't agree with the way things went at home. On her sixteenth birthday, I ordered a small sculpture for her present. It depicted an older female kneeling next to a young girl, embracing her. I told Becky it reminded me of the two of us when she was little and I would come home to sing to her. She said she loved it, and I think that moment broke the ice for the strain I had felt between us for the past couple of years.

The day we went to her apartment to collect her things after she died, the first thing I saw was that sculpture sitting on her living room coffee table. Even now, just the thought of seeing that sculpture reminds me of the unspeakable pain I felt at that moment, and it brings tears to my eyes.

Thoughts in Between number 8: Letter to Becky #1

Dear Becky,

I am consumed by the experience of losing you. I am lost; I am alone. I think of you; soft, gentle music is playing in the background. I sit and gaze at your picture, never turning away as if my actions would dishonor your memory; trying not to stare too long for fear of the inevitable flow of tears that will follow. Too late; I'm crying again. I wonder how a body could contain so many tears. They fall at the whisper of your name, the touch of your sweater, the sight of your warm smile in a family photograph. I wonder if you know how much I miss you.

Chapter 9

Our College Experience

After Becky graduated from Central Catholic High School, she wasn't sure where she wanted to attend college initially. She eventually decided that she wanted to attend Bowling Green State University, about twenty-five miles south of Toledo, but by the time she completed her application, she wasn't able to get into BGSU full time in the fall of 1985. So, she decided to attend Owens Technical College, where I worked as the Director of Student Activities and Athletics. She figured she would take some of her general courses there to get them out of the way and save a little money, since Owens was less costly than Bowling Green.

In my position at the college I was responsible for all of the programming for students, as well as overseeing the athletic programs. I hired students to work in the department to handle a variety of tasks assigned by me or my assistant, Michael. I was in need of a couple of new student staff members, and I invited Becky to join the staff. She was required to apply just as any other student was and had to meet the criteria for the position. She easily qualified for the job, and she was hired to work ten to fifteen hours a week in the Student Activity Center, where most of our programming took place. Not surprisingly, the students loved her, the other staff loved her, and I was thrilled to have her working in my department. I didn't see her every day, but usually three or four days a week. There were times when it was challenging to have my little sister reporting to me, but honestly, the work was easy and her work ethic made it even easier.

It was fun planning activities and handling the little issues that came up with students participating in our activities. I knew Becky wouldn't be at Owens more than one academic year, so I wanted to enjoy the experience as much as possible. Right after the first of the year, Michael assumed the task of organizing the spring break trip to Florida. I confess I went to Florida as a chaperone several years before, but after the experience, I swore I'd never do that again. I took the opportunity to go for free as a chaperone, but I decided after that trip, I would always pay for any vacation I would take. A free trip wasn't worth the stress of overseeing college students on a spring break trip to Daytona Beach, Florida!

However, as the New Year began and the students started talking about the big spring break trip to Florida, Becky got caught up in the excitement. She had gone to Florida once before with her good friend Melanie, and they had had a great time. They did some crazy things I heard, like hanging out with beach drifters and getting sunburned and drinking way too much for a teenager, or for anyone, for that matter. But, she said she would do things differently this time. Would I like to go? Becky invited our sister Mary to travel with her, and she invited me and Marsha to go as well. We also invited my friend Lorinda, the Registrar of the college, to travel with us. With five of us in the traveling party and staying in one room, we cut the cost way down per person. So, we all headed to Florida for that twenty-two hour drive in Lorinda's car, with our luggage stuffed in the trunk and partially on our laps. We met my good friend Chris, a dental hygiene instructor at Owens, in Florida. He was staying with a friend a few miles away, but joined us most every day for food and fun.

We took turns sleeping on the floor, since there were only two double beds. It didn't really matter, because we could sleep on the beach or by the pool. Becky and Mary spent a lot of time sunbathing and drawing all kinds of attention from the guys who were there, and they enjoyed it. I know that we went there as friends, but I couldn't help be the big sister and keep an eye on them and all the attention they were getting. They were both beautiful women, and although their projected aloofness was fun to watch, I found myself hovering over them more than I should have. One evening mid-week, I hadn't seen Mary all day and I was getting concerned. Becky was hanging out with a couple of the Owens students that afternoon and wasn't sure where she was either. When she finally joined us in the early evening, I demanded to know where she had been. Didn't she know that there was danger out there with all of those horny, drunk guys drooling over her? Mary responded pretty indifferently, without getting too bothered by my comments or behavior, but Becky made an observation:

"I didn't know Mother Theresa came to Florida with us," she belted out.

As soon as she said that, I realized I had been hawking them on their vacation, as if I were their mother, not their protective sister and friend.

"Wow, I guess you are right," I apologized sheepishly.

"If I do that again, feel free to call me Mother Theresa," I finished.

As much as I learned my lesson, I still had to bite my tongue at times throughout the remainder of the trip. I guess I should have been honored to be compared to the kind and loving Sister, but I don't think that was Becky's intention. At any rate, she reminded me to trust them both, and that was the end of Mother Theresa.

The rest of the week went by quickly. We ended up doing some of the same crazy things we each did the last time we went to Florida, like drinking too much, hanging out with some drifters, and getting sunburned. But we had a great time, and we laughed about all the memories we created all the way home.

Thoughts in Between number 9

Thoughts of the violence have ravaged my brain and left my heart floating in a pool of misery. It drifts aimlessly, resting only when my mind escapes to well-earned slumber at night, only to awaken to the pain of another day without you. It starts again . . .

CHAPTER 10

The Cottage

In 1983, Dani and George arranged with my parents to purchase a small cottage up in Hillsdale County, Michigan, on Cub Lake. It was a relatively small lake, joined by two other smaller lakes in the southeastern corner of the county. About an hour and fifteen minute drive from Toledo, the cottage was an easy destination for a weekend getaway. Although the cottage was a bit of a fixer upper, it was a great place to go from April to September.

The inside of the cottage left a little bit to be desired, with all of the original furniture in place in the living room. Two old, stiff couches were nestled across from one another at the front window, and a third lounger type piece was across the room, about five feet away. The kitchen had hardly any room for more than one person to work at the stove at a time, and the bathroom with the bare necessities of a toilet and sink meant that any needed body cleansing would have to be done in the lake water. Two bedrooms completed the upper level.

The cottage rested on the slope of a gradual hill heading down towards the lake. Beneath the main area was a large open room, accessible only from the outside staircase. All of the inner tubes, fishing rods, lounge chairs, and other accessories were stored in the rear of the room. With little room to spare, a large table was centered in the remaining space. Often in the evenings, after the small kids were put to bed, the rest of us would pull out the board games and play for hours.

Sometimes on a cool evening, George would get a fire going in the pit out near the big weeping willow tree. Instead of gathering inside, we would sit around the campfire, talking, laughing, drinking a few beers, and mostly just enjoying the atmosphere. On occasion, I would bring my guitar with me for the weekend, but I usually didn't sit and play when my brothers were there, since they were into very different music—rock, alternative, anything that wasn't too mellow or pensive. When we were all there, games in the lower level were usually the activity of choice. But I remember a September evening when Becky came into town without Richard, and Mom, Dani, George, their girls, and Marsha and I were the only ones up for the weekend.

With Dani and George putting the kids to bed, and Mom inside reading, Marsha, Becky and I sat down around the fire George had built. I pulled out my guitar and started playing some of my favorite tunes. Becky and Marsha sang along to some and other times just sat and enjoyed the ambience. After awhile, Marsha headed up to bed, and Becky and I were left alone at the fire.

"I remember when you used to come home from college and sing to me," she revealed.

"I always looked forward to that," she continued, "and I always loved the fact that you would come and spend time with a dumb little kid instead of doing something else," she finished.

"You did so much for me, Lis. You were *my hero*, you know?" she said fondly as she leaned over to hug me. I was speechless for a few moments. What a profound statement to make to someone who often felt pretty inadequate at most things.

"Becky," I slowly began, "I am so honored that you would think that. I really don't know what to say," I muttered.

"Well, it's true. Mom and Dad were always so busy with everything and everyone. You were always there for me, and I've always looked up to you," she claimed as she took her last drink from the can.

Her words were so powerful, and I was humbled by her remarks. They made me recall so many memories of those times, and I felt so proud to have such stature in someone's eyes. Still, I became instantly aware of the tremendous responsibility of being someone's hero and how extremely important it was to project a conscientious and decent persona in front of young people. Sure, I probably knew deep inside that I needed to be a good role model to my younger siblings, but I guess it never really hit me until she actually spoke those words.

That conversation was deeply embedded in my brain, and I thought not only about Becky's comments, but about the whole notion of heroes. As much as I wanted to, I couldn't really relate to her admiration of a hero. I realized I couldn't identify one individual I considered a hero in my own life. Maybe my grandfather on my mother's side, but he had been gone over 20 years. Maybe I just got older and close minded to the idea of having a hero, someone to look up to, someone to model my own behavior after. I was at a loss over that, and the thought of actually being someone's hero burned even deeper inside of me.

I didn't stop thinking about that for a long time.

Thoughts in Between number 10

I find myself lost in music a lot. In particular, there's one song that reminds me of Becky. It reminds me of a dream I had of her, and it strikes me as no other song does, even though there are countless songs that remind me of her. There are no words, but the second it begins I have vivid images of her coming and going into my mind. It grips me and freezes me in space, making me feel lifeless and numb. An incredible chill races up and down my spine, and my torso shakes uncontrollably. The only other motion of my entire body is the desperate gaze from eyes, darting left and right, searching for a glimpse of her. Ever so slowly, I find her picture across the room, with her beautiful smile and loving face. Instantly, my eyes pool with tears and mask my view until I can see nothing. I turn away, wiping the tears, looking for a window or a door, desperately hoping to see her there, in the drive, across the street, through the trees. I am so disappointed that she doesn't magically appear. In pain and filled with sadness, I close my eyes. Only then, with the soft, almost eerie melody reaching deep in my soul and capturing my entire being, do I see her face, hear her voice, and imagine her touch to my hand. This is where I find her, when the music consumes me and takes me far away from the reality of missing her.

CHAPTER 11

Living With Becky

I n 1989, I was living in a duplex with Marsha in west Toledo while we were saving money to buy a house in a couple of years. Dani and George had built their home in Sylvania Township about seven years before and had recently decided to put it on the market. They had their two small girls, Caitlin and Hanna, with a third child on the way. Although their home was once nestled out away from developments and heavy traffic, things were changing. Construction of a neighborhood development just across Centennial Road on the east side of their property was well underway. A noticeable increase in traffic led to a number of accidents at their corner. They decided to move their family into Sylvania, where they bought a small house that rested a hundred and fifty yards from the street. They would have plenty of room to add on and plenty of safe distance from the road for the kids to play.

A few months into this plan, the four of us had been visiting and we mentioned how we were saving to eventually buy a house.

"Why don't you buy our house?" George asked us.

"We can't afford a house right not," I replied. "But if we could, we'd buy yours. We love your house." I continued.

"You could buy it on land contract," George explained.

He gave us some options on buying their home through a land contract, where we would pay rent during the first year, with a small portion of our monthly payment going towards a down payment. At the end of the first year, we would proceed to get financing to purchase the house. After a lot of discussions, we decided to buy their house.

At the time Dani and George were preparing their move, Becky lived with them. As they spoke of their impending move, Marsha and I decided to invite Becky to live with us. A little rent money from her would help with the monthly payments we weren't yet accustomed to, and our new house had plenty of room. I thought it would be great to get reacquainted with Becky again, and to be able to spend quality time with her on a regular basis. I figured it would work out perfectly!

However, we experienced a few glitches in the process of moving, some that strained all of our relationships. The biggest problem arose when the duplex was rented in late November, and we planned to move into our new house on Bancroft. Unfortunately, although Dani and George intended to move into their new place at the same time, their move was delayed until after Christmas. Since we had to get out of the duplex and they had no place to go, we moved into their guest room, and put many of our things into half of their garage. For the next six weeks, five adults and two small children lived in the house on Bancroft. The house that once seemed spacious and comfortable was suddenly crowded and challenging. Dani, pregnant with Cecelia, was having a terrible time with morning sickness and was routinely miserable and cranky. She and George were trying to get organized with their belongings, packing as much as possible, while the girls were buzzing around with all the changes. Plus, the Christmas season was in full swing. It was a pretty crazy time for all of us.

Throughout this time, Becky was working for Lucas County Family and Children's Services as a child sexual abuse investigator. Her encounters with alleged perpetrators had Dani and me nervous a lot of the time, worried about when she would get home, if she was safe, and wondering what kind of people she had to deal with every day. She traveled into poor neighborhoods that were often infested with gangs and drug activity. George had equipped her with a can of mace, but I don't know that she would have ever used it. She insisted she was always fine, and I worried that she trusted people a little too much.

Throughout this period, little Hanna was developing an exceptional temperament. She had tantrums regularly, sometimes daily, often for no apparent reason. She had her fits with her sister Caitlin, her mom and dad, even Marsha and me once. In between packing, the pregnancy, and the crabby kids, Marsha and I would often retreat to our little corner of the house, which had been Dani's sewing room. We had a couple of boxes of clothes, a mattress on the floor, and Becky to help keep us sane at times.

It sometimes seemed like a three ring circus during those weeks, although there were times when the experiences were delightfully priceless. My favorite memory was decorating the Christmas tree with everyone in the house. Dani, George and the girls hung their ornaments on one half of the tree, while Marsha and I decorated the other half. The girls strung icicles all over their half in little clumps of sparkling silver, while I meticulously placed ours in very neat fashion. Since she was a part of both families, Becky cheerfully placed her ornaments on both sides, poetically reminding us of the spirit of all coming together at Christmas. It was probably the most unique and beautiful Christmas tree I'd ever seen.

When Marsha and I bought the house from Dani and George, Becky had already been living in the room over the master bedroom. Her room was rather spacious, and it had a unique feel to it. Maybe it was the way she decorated it, or maybe it was because it had been an attic space converted into a usable living space. Regardless, it was her sanctuary, and she liked it just fine. When Marsha and I first moved into the house before Christmas, we shared the guest room at the top of the stairs. When Dani, George and the girls moved out, we moved into the girls' bed room, which was much larger and across the hall from Becky's. We had decided that we would leave the master bedroom downstairs as our music room, where we could spread out all of the sound equipment, keyboards, and guitars and have room to practice our dancing too.

Being from a large family, I was quite used to sharing space with others, whether it was bedrooms, bathrooms, or any living space, for that matter. I had had lots of roommates over the years, in college and afterwards, but this was the first time since I had moved out of my parents' home when I went away to college that I was once again sharing my space with a family member. Still, I wasn't really worried about living with Becky, because we had gotten closer over the past few years, and especially since she had moved in with Dani and George about 5 or 6 months earlier. Even though she was thirteen years younger than I was, I knew we would get along okay.

As we settled into our new living arrangements, I soon learned that I gained so much more than a new roommate. Becky and I shared many values, attitudes and our outlook on life. I realized that in many ways, we were very much alike, and our friendship grew tighter. We enjoyed much of the same music, and what we hadn't shared before, we quickly grew to appreciate. I was always a big John Denver fan, but I liked a lot of other folksy music, too. I enjoyed a wide variety of music styles, and in the past couple of years, I had developed a fondness for some classical pieces. In particular, I loved Pachelbel's Canon in D. I shared Denver and Pachelbel with Becky, and she shared Michael W. Smith, Kim Hill, and other Christian artists with me. One fond image I have of her is of her lying on the living room sofa, having fallen asleep with Pachelbel still playing in the background. She was snuggled up in her gray and white striped flannel pajamas looking sweet and innocent, without a care in her head. I thought for a second she looked like an angel.

Becky, Marsha and I all liked the tunes of Amy Grant. Although she had transitioned from Christian music to the pop scene in the last couple of years, we all liked her voice and the things she sang about. Honestly, I never really appreciated any kind of religious affiliated music, but I found Amy Grant's music charming and simple, with just a hint of girl-next-door warmth that struck a chord with me. Becky was quite passionate about her Christian music, and she loved it as much as anything else.

Later that spring, Amy Grant came to Toledo for a concert. Without hesitation about the cost, we ordered tickets as soon as they became available. We got seats less than twenty rows from the stage. What a thrill! As a special bonus, Kim Hill was featured as her opening act. Unbelievable! Although I wasn't that familiar with her music, after the concert, I was sold on it. And Becky sang along to every word. I could just tell by watching her, beaming as she sang along, that she was in heaven. And once Amy took the stage, the place was rocking like nothing I had ever seen before. She sang several of her recent radio hits, such as *Baby, baby*, and most of the audience were on their feet, bopping to her catchy melodies. But then, she broke into one of her more popular Christian songs, *Everywhere I Go*. As the song began, Becky did her trademark clapping, hands slapping together vigorously. She was so excited! She began swaying back and forth, with both arms raised in the air, singing at the top of her lungs. She was singing praise, loving life, and basking in the pleasure of the experience. I just stood next to her, swaying to her rhythm, watching her with such admiration and joy. It was such a touching moment for me. I hope it never leaves my memory.

Becky had such a passion for caring for others, and it was never more evident than in the job she had at the time. Her primary task was to get to the root of accusations and charges of abuse, most often in the child's home. Still, after spending about a year and a half with the agency, the stress of the job took its toll, and she decided she would leave Lucas County Family and Children's Services and find something else. I don't know if it was the challenges of confronting often hostile individuals or the frustration of not being able to do enough for the kids that led her to her decision. But I've known many people in community service social work, and I've seen lots of them get burned out. I think Becky just needed to move on to new challenges where she could feel a sense of satisfaction in making a difference in peoples' lives.

Throughout a good portion of her college years at Lourdes, Becky worked as a hostess and waitress at a couple of the Lebanese restaurants in town. She first worked at a place called *The Beirut* on the west side of Toledo and then switched to *Byblos* in the south end. Byblos was opened by the same family that owned *The Beirut*. The head chef and part owner, Ziad, was moving over to the new restaurant, and Becky loved working with him, so she followed him. She continued to work there sparingly while at Children's Services Bureau, and once she left the agency, she began working more hours at the restaurant.

Many times she would come home after work, stains splattered on her clothing, with great stories of her experiences of the day. She would talk about fattoush, tabouli, hummus, and baklava, all Middle Eastern menu items. She would giggle as she recalled her customers' difficulties in pronouncing the entrees correctly.

"Today I asked this guy if he wanted any dessert," she said with a smirk on her face.

You could see she was quite amused.

"And then he said, I would like some of this *Bot Lay Wah*, and it was all I could do to keep from laughing," she finished. The baklava or *Bot Lay Wah* story got a lot of mileage in our house for quite some time after that.

Becky and Ziad had a wonderful friendship. I know that Ziad was very fond of Becky, as she was of him. He was a gracious gentleman, and I remember when we first went into the restaurant and Becky introduced us; he was very shy, but very kind. He bought us a coffee drink on the house, which he often did any other time I ate at his establishment. To this day, Ziad still shows the same kindness and warmth whenever I eat at *Byblos*. And although his life is very different these days, with a wife and two kids of his own, I know Becky left a lasting impression on him. After all this time, a smiling picture of her still rests on the back counter where the waitresses gather, a gentle reminder of a beautiful spirit that shared some time there.

In addition to working at the restaurant, Becky got a job as a Youth Minister at Lutheran Church Of Our Savior in West Toledo. This was a part-time job that gave her the opportunity to work in a more positive setting with kids and also an avenue to share her deep faith and convictions. A few times a week, Becky would head over to the church to plan activities, meet with the teenagers from the church, and do her best to influence their spiritual sides. Most of these kids were from decent families and neighborhoods, and they responded to her favorably. She was young, extremely likable, and highly energetic. She organized car washes, picnics, short trips, and even gatherings at our house on Bancroft for pizza or a movie. She poured her self into this job, investing so much more than she was ever paid for. But she loved working with young people.

Initially, when she first accepted the position, I thought it was weird that she would work for a Lutheran Church. After all, based on what I was taught in Catholic grade school, the Catholic Church was really the only church and the one true religion; anything else was less. But when I shared these thoughts with Becky, she reminded me in her insightfulness that fundamentally, it's all about God. It doesn't really matter what church you attend to pray, what's most important is that you pray. And you believe. And you live your life to the best of your ability. She never ceased to amaze me with her wisdom. How did she know these things? Where did all this sensitivity and understanding come from? She was, after all, only twenty-two years old when she took this job. She truly had a remarkable spirit.

Thoughts in Between number 11

The "good life" is behind me now. Oh sure; I've got plenty of memories of happy times, fun, joy and laughter to take with me on the rest of my journey. And I've got the most important treasures—family and friends—to sustain me along the way. But, it's time to get to work, to get busy. I've been lucky; I've lived so fully these last forty years. But the fun and the happiness isn't so important any more. No, I've got to get busy, got to get to work. I've got to find the answer to that burning question: What am I still doing here? That is my task, to search, to delve, to ponder. Only when I find the answer, or perhaps, when the answer finds me, can I go back to the fun, the joy, and the laughter. And, it feels like it will be a long journey.

CHAPTER 12

Maiden America and Becky

As far back as I can remember, I have always enjoyed playing the guitar. When I was thirteen, I asked for a guitar for Christmas. I figured since Rick had the opportunity to take organ lessons during his eighth grade year, and my father had bought a beautiful organ for both my mom and Rick to play and practice the year before, a little, hand held guitar wouldn't be too much to ask for. I guess I was wrong. When I opened the large wrapped gift on Christmas day back in 1966, I was sorely disappointed to uncover a plastic, junior sized guitar. Sure, it had nylon strings, but it wasn't exactly what I had hoped for.

Nonetheless, I plunked on that thing until my senior year of high school when a neighbor kid was selling his old guitar for ten bucks. I bought it, and thus began my folk music career. Throughout the next several years, I taught myself how to play chords, mostly plinking away at John Denver tunes. I bought a couple of better guitars during that time, and spent many afternoons and evenings strumming with friends, singing and playing, as if there wasn't a thing to do but play music.

When Marsha and I got together in 1984, I was delighted that she played the piano. She admitted she didn't play that well, but I wasn't very good either, so we were a perfect fit. I knew it was time to follow one of my many dreams to start a band, and so we did. We had two other musical friends who were eager to get things going too. We cleverly named ourselves "Maiden America," in recognition that we were all single females, and it was just such a catchy name! We played for about a year and a half before one of our members got transferred to second shift work, and there went the end of our band. I was depressed over it for several months, and decided to take some guitar lessons in hopes of improving my playing skills. Hell, I didn't even know how to read music, so anything would be an improvement. Stephanie worked at one of the local music stores, where I bought my equipment. She offered to teach me guitar techniques and how to read music. I took lessons from her for about six months, when out of the blue, she asked if Marsha and I were interested in starting up a band again. It was a moment I had been waiting so long for. We started rehearsals, twice a week, alternating between our house and Steph's house. We were much more disciplined and within six months, we began playing out at clubs. Over the next few years we played often and wherever we could get gigs, from bars to yacht clubs, from schools to private parties. We even traveled to New York City a couple of times to play for an educational organization Marsha's mother belonged to. When Marsha and I bought Dani and George's house, we set up the master bedroom as our studio and practiced there, still two times a week. With Becky's bedroom right over the master, she heard our rehearsals every Wednesday and Friday, whether she liked it or not.

We played an eclectic range of music, including pop, Motown, early rock and roll, ballads, and a few original pieces. Thanks to the latest technology in the keyboard, we were able to download all kinds of instrument sounds and create a full band sound with drums, horns, and strings, even though there were only three of us playing at one time.

Many times, we were busy working out harmonies and arrangements when Becky would pop into the room to sing along or just to listen. I'll never forget once when we were playing and singing *Celebration,* by Kool and the Gang. The song was loud and full of downloaded horns and percussion in addition to our own instrument contributions, and the major part of the chorus was spiked with high cries of "woo hoo," which all of us sang together. We were in the middle of the song just shouting out a round of the "woo hoos" when Becky came strutting into the room, singing "woo hoo" at the top of her lungs. She danced around the room as if she were on a stage, singing demonstratively until she couldn't keep from laughing any more. We all laughed right along with her, letting the programmed sounds continue even though the real musicians in the room had stopped playing. She really was a good sport about the whole set up, but I knew she had her fun with it too.

Thoughts in Between number 12: Letter to Becky #2

Dear Becky,

I think of you now and the tears fill my eyes as I look back on the times we spent together. You shared so much with so many others that I know I cannot claim those treasured moments as my own. But here in my house, they belong to me. I see you lying on my blue couch, looking warm and snuggly in those gray and white striped pajamas, listening to Pachelbel's Canon In D. I see you reading a book or maybe catching a quick nap.

I stare in my kitchen and see you at the table as you smile at me and say, "this looks great," in admiration of the meal I've prepared. We join hands and give thanks for the many blessings God has given us and then gently squeeze our grip before letting go to eat. I always laughed as you bounced into the room where the band rehearsed, each time we'd sing "Celebration" by Kool and the Gang. You'd chime in with the "woo hoos," and we'd all get a kick out of it. It took me so long to sing that song again.

I remember your brown Bass shoes sitting by the doorway for a month, waiting for you to retrieve them on your next visit home. When you left them here at my house at Christmas time and picked them up on January 31st, who would know they would leave such a memory etched in my mind? When we cleaned your apartment, I found those shoes, and I cried as I clutched them close to my heart. They weren't just shoes anymore, but a part of you and my life with you.

CHAPTER 13

Sharing A Secret

Even though Becky and I were really close, I was never really forthcoming about my lifestyle. It wasn't doing any harm keeping it from her, so I figured it was best to leave things unsaid. But one night we decided to go out for drinks and to listen to a local band playing at a club in the south end of Toledo. Becky's good friend Melanie, Marsha, Becky and I were all having a good time talking, laughing and enjoying the music when Becky pointed her finger at me to pull me closer to her.

"I thought we were close enough that you could be truthful with me," she rather scolded me as she continued.

"When I was housesitting for you I pulled out some photo albums and I saw some pictures I hadn't seen before . . . , I see that you and Marsha had a ceremony!"

She wasn't angry but very firm in her tone. I wasn't sure what to expect next.

"I saw that Dani was there; you never asked me to be there! Why would you hide this from me? Such a special day in your life and you kept it a secret!" She finished.

I was shocked and totally caught off guard.

"I didn't know how you felt about it, and you know, not everyone supports these kinds of relationships. Would you have wanted to come?" I asked.

"Of course I would have! I went to Dani's wedding and Sara's; why wouldn't I want to come to yours?" she continued.

"I think it's stupid that people can't love who they want to love or who they might fall in love with," she added.

I just smiled at her, and then gave her as big of a hug as I could from across the table. She was amazing, so honest and so good, and I felt badly that I had excluded her from the commitment ceremony that Marsha and I had had a couple years before. We invited just a few close friends, and since Dani was one of my closest friends, of course I invited her. I appreciated Becky's acceptance. That experience made me feel even closer to her, and I really admired her for her openness and encouragement . . . just one more thing that made her so special.

October 27, 1997 A letter to myself

I don't think I ask for much. I live simply, I respect the earth and those that inhabit her. I believe that all persons are equal and worthy of a fair chance at not only survival but success, and I believe in the natural order of life's cycle, namely: that we are all put here in this place to live, learn, grow, contribute, challenge, embrace, and honor every living being, appreciating the place we each have in this world and accepting the value of one being equal to the other. We live, we give, we let go, and so it continues. I know that I am but a small piece of this fabric of humanity. Probably in years to come I will barely be remembered. If I have done my duty to destiny and if I have given the most I can give, I might be remembered. But it's not for the future that I toil; it's not for the world in years ahead that I struggle and yearn for something more. I believe that my destiny is here and now; whatever difference I can make must be made now.

And so, it's true: I don't ask for much, but maybe two things: the first, most essentially, is the freedom to follow my heart, to understand the direction that my life must travel and the ability to do so; and secondly, peace of mind, which comforts me on my journey, telling me I am doing exactly what I have been called to do.

Thoughts in Between number 13

In a crowded room of smiling, eager faces, I am alone.

In the stores, in the malls, in a packed auditorium, I am alone.

On the city streets in the thick of rush hour, I am alone.

At the church where the choir sings those old Polish songs, I am alone.

On the field, in the gym, walking through the woods, I am alone.

In that place of my heart I've saved just for you, I am most alone.

Without the chance to share anything and everything with you, I feel so lonely.

I don't mind being alone, but being lonely is something I can't bear.

And in that place I've saved just for you, I am so lonely without you there.

CHAPTER 14

Becky The Dancer

Becky loved to dance. When she was a young girl, she liked to dance around the living room with my mom and sometimes, with my father. When she was quite young, he would have her stand on his feet, facing him, while he held her hands. He would move about the room to the music playing, usually to his favorite polkas on Sunday mornings, with her giggling and bobbing along. My dad did that with me, and I suppose he shared that little bit of fun with my other sisters too. We were too small and he was very particular about his polkas to just bounce around the room without regard to the beat or melody. I guess I remember Becky dancing with him, because by that time, I was too old, or felt too old to be standing on my father's feet and letting him do the dancing for me. But Becky loved it. I'll bet that's when her love of Polish music first started.

While Becky was in high school, she got involved in a few of the school's musicals. She never had any lead or major roles, but she did participate in the choruses of some of the shows. I'm sorry to say that I don't remember her high school performances, but I saw the photographs my mom took. I recall one picture where she was smiling, all dressed up in costume, with her arms raised in the air. She was a little out of sync with the girls next to her, but who knew by the photos who was right on the beat and who wasn't?

Later in her high school years, she learned a lot of dance moves from her good friend Melanie. Melanie took dance lessons for so many years that it was second nature to her to feel the beat of a song and move to it. Being her best friend for so many years, Becky learned a lot of routines and dance styles. She loved going out dancing, often with Melanie or other friends.

I wasn't really that familiar with her abilities on the dance floor until an evening out with her, my sister Mary, Marsha, and Stephanie from our band. We went to a bar that I don't even remember the name of, to hear a couple of local musicians play. We had a few drinks, sat and laughed a lot, and enjoyed the music. At one point, the duo started singing a Paula Abdul song called *"Word Up."* I was not fond of the tune, but when Mary and Becky got up out of their seats to bop and get funky to its beat, I found myself watching the two of them instead of the two singing the song. They were the only two on the dance floor, and so most eyes in the room turned to them. They took advantage of the spotlight, so to speak, and over exaggerated their moves, all in fun. Nothing against Mary, but Becky was really going to town with the stomping and jerking, and hip swiveling. Marsha, Steph and I laughed about our own personal entertainment the rest of the evening. I loved the fact that they were both so uninhibited and able to get up in front of strangers and have that kind of fun. I think Mary let loose because it was easy to do with Becky, and much easier to do when she'd had a couple of drinks. Becky, on the other hand, seemed to do it with ease. She followed her own soul, danced to the beat of her own drum. I thought it was courageous and charming at the same time.

A couple of months after Becky moved to Kalamazoo, Steph, Marsha and I decided to try to put together a medley of three songs where we didn't play any instruments, but danced to the tunes as we sang them. Marsha had some experience in dance from her high school years, but as we tried to create our own routines, we realized we were going to need help. We agreed that Becky would be the perfect helper with this task.

In March of 1991 the family headed up to Adrian to celebrate Mark T's birthday. I had made arrangements to bring a cassette player along with my video camera, and Becky would listen to the songs and work with Marsha and me to come up with some dance moves that we could use with our medley.

After some birthday celebrating, the three of us went into the hall upstairs, and I set up my camera while Marsha manned the music.

Becky stood in the hall just in front of the bathroom. The hall was small, giving Becky about a 4 by 6 foot space to dance and twirl and show her moves. She didn't disappoint us.

The medley started with the catchy, strutting song, "Can't Stop," and ended with the lively playful tune, "I Wanna Be Rich." Becky listened briefly to the songs, one by one, while stepping, swaying, motioning her arms, and clapping her hands with bursts of energy. She ad-libbed here and there, causing all three of us to break into laughter that almost brought tears to my eyes. Marsha practiced some of her steps and moves with her in hopes of being able to remember them to teach Steph and me. We spent nearly an hour upstairs with Becky, singing, laughing, and making mental notes. If we could duplicate some of her suggestions and dance half as well as she did, we could pull off this medley without too much embarrassment. Becky made it look so easy and so fun that I wanted to dance like her, even though I knew the odds of that happening weren't all that great. But she was a great sport for helping us, and the tapes from that afternoon are treasures I'll never part with.

THOUGHTS IN BETWEEN NUMBER 14: LETTER TO BECKY #3

Dear Becky,

When I see you again will you recognize my face, or will the years in between put doubts inside your mind? All the years of living I've been through run faint within my soul. So many years have come and gone since you've gone away, though it seems like only yesterday my world was shattered. It doesn't seem to matter how many days have passed; the aching and the desperation are the only things that last. Good times, well, they come and go, but they never stay long. Instead, the memories of your lost life burn clearly and ever so strongly.

CHAPTER 15

Angels Watching Over Her

There were three times that Becky's life was threatened, but she managed to escape them without severe bodily harm. The first time occurred when she was just about eight. It was a warm summer evening, and I decided to call my mom to see how things were back in Toledo. I had just graduated from Siena Heights and was working up in Adrian. Answering the phone on the other end was my brother Steve.

"Hey Steve, how are you?" I asked.

After a brief exchange, I requested to speak with Mom.

"She's at the hospital," he replied without pause or explanation.

I was puzzled because her third shift wasn't due to begin for at least three hours.

"Why is she at the hospital so early?" I pressed him for a reply. "Because of the accident," he exclaimed.

"What accident?" I cried out.

He proceeded to tell me that my sister Dani had been with her college friend Ruth and the three youngest kids—Mary, Joey and Becky. They were involved in a car accident but he didn't have any details. I was frantic and raced to find my girlfriend Maureen to rush down to Flower Hospital just outside Toledo.

When we arrived, I first found Mary and Joey sitting in a waiting area, banged up but otherwise okay. Moments later I found Ruth, who was visibly shaken but unhurt. Dani was nearby with a broken nose, bruised and swollen twice its normal size. After initially being relieved to find the four of them shaken but fortunately okay, I realized that someone was missing from the waiting area.

"Where's Mom? Where's Becky?" I nervously asked.

Dani pointed me around the corner to a separate room. Becky was lying on a bed, Mom hovering over her, holding her hand. Apparently, she had bounced around the car, and was being treated for a skull fracture, along with a concussion. Trying desperately to hide my fear, I cuddled her, adding my efforts to soothe her. She wasn't crying and although I could tell she was scared, she was somewhat calm for a kid who was laid out in an unfamiliar place with doctors and nurses coming in and out to see her. I knew I had to be strong for her, but she seemed to be the one who was strong that night.

Apparently, they were all coming back from swimming at Bowman Pool, about fifteen minutes from Birckhead. Ruth was crossing Berdan Avenue when a car, traveling at a high speed, crashed into hers. The impact was so intense that it spun Ruth's car around completely, sending it to land across the intersection, through a fence, and into a yard. A post from the corner of the fence spiked its way into the passenger side open window. Fortunately for Dani, the impact sent her forward into the dashboard, where she smashed her nose. Had she been restrained in her seat, the fence post would have likely pierced through her head. Mary and Joey were on the opposite side of the impact and banged to the back seat floor. Becky's side was hit, and she suffered the brunt of the crash. She was kept overnight for observation, and thankfully, experienced no repercussions from the accident. I really don't know how it affected her psychologically, but she never let on that it bothered her much afterwards. I know Ruth felt terribly guilty, and Mom was noticeably distraught. As for me, I didn't want her or Joe or Mary, for that matter, riding in a car anytime soon. But life goes on, and a short time later they were back at the pool having fun like little kids should.

The second time she was involved in a life threatening close call was when she attended Owens Technical College and worked for me in the Student Activities and Athletics Department. One afternoon in late fall, a student came into the Hall and nervously told me that there had been an accident on the expressway. It was a small black car very much like the one Becky drove. The student thought it might have been her but couldn't be sure because traffic was backed up on the highway to where he couldn't really get a good view of the accident scene.

He said that from what he heard, another car, one twice the size of the black one, had tried to merge onto the freeway, not hesitating for any other oncoming traffic. The road was rather congested at the time of day, and all lanes were full. The black car was in the right lane, and the oversized vehicle sped forward, nudging the little black subcompact. Apparently the driver of the smaller car tried desperately to control it as it teetered from the impact, but it quickly rolled over on its roof, with the driver hanging upside down, restricted by the safety belt secured over her shoulder.

I ran into my office and threw on my coat, yelling to Michael, my assistant, as he looked at me, puzzled by my behavior. I didn't have time to explain, and maybe it wasn't Becky, but I knew she had just left campus. A gut wrenching feeling scared me, and I knew I had to go see for myself. As I approached the entrance ramp to the expressway, I could see that cars were backed up ahead for several hundred yards. I pulled onto the shoulder and slowly drove forward. About a hundred yards from the flashing red lights at the scene, a policeman motioned for me to stop. I rolled down my window and before he could say anything, I pleaded with him.

"That's my sister up there! I've got to go see if she's alright!" I blurted out.

Surprisingly, he ushered me forward along the shoulder. By the time I got to the scene, the black car had been turned back upright. Standing nearby was Becky. It was her!

"Becky! Are you okay?"

I rushed to her and squeezed her tightly before pulling back and examining her for any injuries. She looked a bit rattled, but otherwise seemed fine. Her car had some serious dents and creases from flipping upside down, but she appeared relatively calm for a person who just got slammed into and turned upside down.

"I'm okay," she said reassuringly. "It scared the crap out of me at first, but the seat belt saved my life," she continued.

A lot of people don't wear seat belts, especially younger people who have a feeling of invincibility behind the wheel of a car. Thank God Becky was as sensible as she was! She tried to do the right thing most of the time, which is a trait many of us inherited from my father.

She explained that she was fine and didn't need to go to the hospital. She was concerned about the other driver who sped away in a hurry. A witness to the accident got the license plate number, and we later learned that the owner of the car was an inner city resident without insurance. It made Becky angry that her insurance would probably increase, but mostly that someone would leave the scene of an accident without any regard for anyone else. Sometimes she was so naïve, but her innocence was one of the most charming things about her personality. Becky viewed the cruelties of the real world as ridiculously unnecessary, and I think that deepened her sense of justice and her unwavering passion for the disadvantaged and for those she believed were treated unfairly.

The third time Becky faced a terrifying danger was when she lived with Marsha and me on Bancroft. One Friday night the band was rehearsing as usual, when we heard the door slam. We stopped to listen but there was silence. Puzzled, I took off my guitar and headed across the house to the side door. Becky was in a panic, pushing the buttons of the alarm system, while hiding away from the door window.

"Becky, what's wrong? What are you doing?" I asked suspiciously.

"There was a gun," she cried in a breathless statement. "A guy pulled into the driveway behind me and asked me for directions," she continued.

"When I turned to put my key into the lock, he made a sound and when I turned around, he had the gun pointing in my face!"

She was frightened and started crying. I quickly called the police and explained the situation to Marsha and Stephanie who had come into the kitchen to see what was going on.

A few minutes later three county police cars pulled into our driveway. Moments later, a state highway patrol car arrived. Becky told them what had happened. She had gotten off work around 9:30 pm and was going to head home. Her boyfriend Richard had met her at work and instead of coming home, they had gone out for pizza. Adjacent to the pizza place was a carryout and Becky wanted to get some pop for home. She kissed Richard goodbye and proceeded to buy her pop and head for home. Apparently, a couple of guys had seen her say goodbye to her boyfriend and then followed her home. They pulled into the driveway behind her, and the passenger stumbled out of the car. Becky could tell that he was either drunk or high, but she dismissed any thoughts about danger when he asked her for directions. She used the hood of the car to draw a map of where they were and where they said they wanted to go. She told him good luck and turned to enter the house. He took the 45 pistol out from his pants and pointed it in her face as she turned around. He wanted all of her money. She was scared to death and nervously told him she didn't have any. He asked her if she thought he was kidding and fired a shot into the air. Again she said she didn't have any money because her purse was inside, but she would go and get it for him. He was getting angrier by the second and threatened to shoot her. He aimed the trigger into the night air to fire it again, but somehow it jammed. As he fumbled with the gun to see what was wrong, Becky got the key into the lock and managed to get inside. When I approached her, the car was racing out of our drive. It all happened so fast.

She was lucky, and we were all lucky that gun jammed. Who knows what would have happened? The incident scared her for a long time. She was fearful of traveling out alone to the mall, the store, or the park. It scared me too. We were all afraid to go outside the house after dark. It was Memorial weekend and we had just gotten our golden retriever puppy, Bailey. We never let anyone take Bailey out alone in the dark for months. Often we would go out with a baseball bat in our hands, sometimes with the fake rifle George had given us to protect ourselves. Becky thought she saw the gunman once at the mall months later, and it started the fear all over again. After the gun scare, I couldn't help thinking about how Becky's life truly had a special purpose. Most people don't dodge death once, let alone three times, in such a short life. I just knew she was being spared for the greater things down the road.

THOUGHTS IN BETWEEN NUMBER 15

Many of us who knew and loved Becky have tried to make some sense out of what happened to her. We've tried to find a reason, a purpose for her horrific and untimely death. We need to find it for ourselves because we just cannot understand why. But I know that Becky needs no explanation. I read this today:

"Angels live beyond living and dying. Their essence is immortal. Their home is all inclusive, beyond the narrow territories of existence we have defined for ourselves. To an angel, death is not an enemy, but a trip to a new kind of country filled with friends, harmony and comfort. It is a journey with wondrous visions that fill one with love" (author unknown).

And so, I believe that she is an angel, off to another more wonderful existence. I still miss her so very much, and I try my best to keep her alive within me. I am lucky enough to wear her clothes, to feel her wrapped around me when I put on one of her sweaters. I wear her jewelry, in particular, an earring in the shape of a cross. She was wearing it the last time I saw her. I never take it off. I have a couple pairs of her shoes, but I've never worn them, as I don't feel that I could fill the shoes she wore when she was alive. I have the poster she had hanging in her apartment, Rosie the Riveter, the classic depiction of a strong and bold woman during a difficult time in history. I have those pajamas she was wearing the time I took a picture of her after she'd fallen asleep on the couch on Bancroft. She looked like an angel; maybe she was an angel even then. Looking back on that image now, yes, I think she was an angel; I just didn't realize it at the time.

CHAPTER 16

The Five Sisters

I have always felt fortunate to have the family I've got. As I've said, we've all been very close, for as long as I can remember. I think much of it had to do with the fact that we shared tight living space for so many years, and that our parents insisted that we share things, from toys, to clothes, to bedrooms, and to time. Heck, when Dad would call us all together to discipline someone guilty of leaving the lights on or not putting things away, we didn't snitch on one another. Quite often, when no one would come forward to admit a wrongdoing and no one would tell on the other, we'd all get punished. We even shared that.

It's no wonder that we are all so loyal to each other. Growing up without a lot except for each other, we counted on one another for fun, for help, and for support. To this day, I can't imagine not wanting to see any of my siblings on any given day. Sure, we're all independent thinkers and have as many differences as similarities. But I know beyond any doubt that if I needed something from any one of them, I could call and they would be there for me in an instant. It's a bond that I don't think will ever be broken.

Even tighter than the connection between all of us as a family, my sisters and I are interwoven in our souls. It started when we were young, and as each new birth occurred, it continued and remains with us as adults. There we were, Lisa, Dani, Sara, Mary and Becky, always smiling together in all the family photos, always arms wrapped around one another. I suppose it worked out that way early on when Dani, Sara and I were born three girls in a row. We shared a bedroom, and spent hours there singing and talking and playing. We'd get sent to clean our room, and the project that should have taken an hour would last three or four hours, just because we'd stop and sing and laugh and play.

When we moved to Birckhead, the three of us still shared a bedroom, while Mary and Becky shared another room. Although there were many years between all of us when we lived under that one roof, we always got along, always wanted to hang out together. This connection between us is amazing. There's a spiritualness to it, a sensitivity and caring and genuine love that is unparalleled. From the family games where the girls challenged the boys in Family Feud or charades, to the Christmas cookie bake-a-thons we held when we were older, the Binkowski girls have always been a team of nurturing, loving and fun-filled females.

When Mary moved out to California to live with her fiance Scott, it was hard for all of us, but mostly Becky, since they were the closest in age. They had lived together, had some of the same friends, and spent a lot of time together. We threw a going away party for Mary, with the five of us, Marsha, and Mom at our house on Bancroft. We had a great time, eating lots, playing games, drinking a bit, and of course, taking pictures. It was really tough to see her move so far away, and we cherished the trips she made back to Toledo, although they were too infrequent and always too short.

My four sisters have been my closest friends my entire life. I don't know if it's because we grew up taking care of one another or because we spent most of our time outside of school together. Any time I've sorted through the hundreds of pictures I have of my family, I've noticed how the five sisters were often photographed together. Many times Mom was included in those pictures with her girls. Even as adults, at Slowinski gatherings like Christmas, summer picnics, or graduation parties, the Binkowski women would eventually gravitate towards each other. There has always been an inexplicable comfort I've felt in their presence, and I know without a doubt that my sisters all feel the same way. Our friendships with one another are incredible treasures that I wouldn't trade for anything in the world.

Thoughts in Between number 16

The bond I feel with my sisters is something that is priceless, and one of my greatest gifts. When we got the news about Becky, it seems like that bond was frozen in time. It would never be the same. When she died, that picture of the five of us hugging each other, radiating with smiles, would never be repeated. Now, when the family gathers, we still laugh and tell stories, and sometimes have fun. But, we all know something's not quite right because someone is missing. I don't know if I'll ever want a picture taken with the four of us now. I just don't think I can bring myself to do it. God, I miss the five of us.

CHAPTER 17

Moving To Kalamazoo

In the late summer of 1991 Becky was accepted into the Social Work graduate program at Western Michigan University. She had applied to the University of Michigan but didn't get in, so she happily accepted the opportunity to attend WMU, which was located in Richard's home town. She moved out of the house on Bancroft in August to begin her studies and moved into a condo with Richard. In addition to going back to school, it also gave them the chance to be together every day, something they hadn't had before, since their relationship involved a two and a half hour commute except for during late spring and early summer. Richard also studied at WMU, but he owned a commercial fishing boat and, along with his father and brothers, ran fishing tours from spring to mid fall.

Richard started his fishing season on Lake Erie, docked up at Luna Pier, Michigan, about a twenty minute trip up the highway. Becky and Rich met at a pizza place a few years before when he was staying at Luna Pier for a couple of months. In June of each year, he would pull his boat out of Lake Erie and head over to Lake Michigan to run his fishing business there. With the majority of Richard's work season on the west side of Michigan, coupled with his own graduate studies at WMU, Becky's move to Kalamazoo worked out perfectly.

When Becky first moved to Kalamazoo, she worked a couple social work jobs while she went to school full-time. She worked at a group home for adults with developmental disabilities where she spent several hours a week assisting them with assorted tasks. She took them out, too, into town for short excursions just for fun. It was a job she thoroughly enjoyed and a welcome change from the intensity of her job with Family and Children's Services in Toledo.

She also got a job working with a young autistic boy a few hours a week, and this experience helped her decide that she wanted to work with kids once she completed her education. She enjoyed many aspects of the social work field, but she felt working with young people would give her the opportunity to truly make a difference.

While living in Kalamazoo, Becky loved having visitors. She invited her nieces and nephews, brothers and sisters, even our parents, to come to stay with her. I knew she missed her family and although she was pursuing her dreams and her future life with Richard, it was often hard for her to be away from us. When she had the chance, she would come home to Toledo and always stay with me. She was comfortable with Marsha and me, and she was used to the house on Bancroft. When she couldn't make time for a visit, she would encourage people to come to her. I went to her place a couple of times that year, and we had great visits. The first weekend I ever spent with her, I awoke to the smell of something wonderful baking downstairs in the kitchen. She had gotten a recipe for a cream cheese Danish that practically melted in your mouth. Becky wasn't known for her cooking skills, but the things that she did make were delicious, and this was no exception.

I could tell that she was making Kalamazoo her home. She took me into town, then to meet Richard's mom, Robbie, who was quite warm and obviously attached to Becky. I later learned that when Becky and Rich would have their spats, Becky would go talk with Robbie. She was comforting and encouraging, and Becky admired her greatly. On one trip, Becky took Marsha and me to the lake. We walked a long way on the beach, then way out on a pier that stretched several hundred yards into the lake. We sat there and watched the boats come and go, enjoying the warmth of the sun and the soothing sounds of the waves rippling to shore. We told stories, laughing at the silly things we all did, until the sun began to set. Even though we were heading back to her condo, we stood there on the pier and hugged one another, sealing the uneventful but precious time we had shared together.

After her first year in the graduate program of WMU, Becky was offered a position through Family and Children's Services of Kalamazoo to manage a residential facility for mentally ill clients. The complex consisted of two buildings, each with four units in them to house one or two individuals with psychological impairments. The people living in these quarters were assigned by the county mental health department, having been relocated there after residing in either group homes or other restrictive environments. In these apartments, they were given more independence, and Becky's primary responsibility was to assist them with their daily routine to encourage their adaptation to this more open living space. Becky lived in one of the units and Richard stayed with her most of the time. When she was first offered the position, she called me to talk about it. She was excited.

"I think this will be a good experience for me, working with a different population," she told me over the phone.

I could tell she was looking forward to doing something new, but I didn't like it.

"Becky, I'm not so sure this is a good thing for you. Do you really think it's safe?" I asked her point blank.

I had explained to her that I had done a brief internship with mentally ill patients, and I was really uncomfortable with it. I had gotten a Bachelor of Social Work too, and I had been exposed to a variety of people and problems during that period, and working with mentally ill patients was the last kind of job I would have pursued.

"Lis, they wouldn't put these people here if they didn't belong here. I'm sure it will be fine," she defended her choice.

I realized that I was quite judgmental because of my own limited experience, and I didn't say anything else after that. Becky had a really good head on her shoulders, and if she was confident and comfortable, I knew it was wrong for me to try to talk her out of of that job. She was committed to helping people, any people whom she thought she could help. She once sent me a card stating that I was the reason she was doing what she was doing being a social worker and making a difference in the world. She thanked me for being a role model for her. How could I get after her when she said that? I knew I really didn't have the right to keep her from doing what she thought was right for her to do. I doubt that I could have influenced her enough to change her mind anyway. And so she moved into the apartments on Arlington to work with clients with varying mental illnesses. We never talked about the working situation after that, and because she never complained about any of it to me, I assumed everything was going just fine.

February 1, 1995
A letter to the people of Kalamazoo:

It has been two years since the death of my sister, Rebecca Binkowski, who was killed in your community. The past two years have been at the very least, extremely difficult and regularly painful. I'm still trying to make some sense out of all that has happened, to no avail.

Here in Toledo, where she spent most of her life, we will remember her at a memorial service on the anniversary of her death, February 3rd. As much as the events surrounding her murder will be on our minds, it is my hope that the focus at this service will instead be on the many positive ways she touched the lives around her. She gave herself endlessly, trying to make a difference, and I think it's so important that we not lose sight of her life's dedication to doing that. I especially hope that the people of Kalamazoo look beyond the horrors of this tragedy and related events that shook the community that Becky last called home. Instead, I hope you will recall a young, energetic woman with a faith-filled heart and pure love of humanity, an unshakable commitment to social justice, and a deep affection to those she held close in her heart. I'm sure this is how she would like you to remember her.

In her spirit, peace to you.

Thoughts in Between number 17

Often times I think about the path that Becky traveled:

Becky graduated from Central Catholic High School in 1985 and knew that she wanted to pursue a career in a helping profession. Initially interested in psychology, she attended Owens Technical College for a year of general coursework and then transferred to Bowling Green State University. Overwhelmed by the complexity of the campus and the coursework, she left BGSU after one term. She found her educational home at Lourdes College in Sylvania, Ohio, and there she changed her major to Social Work.

Becky found the Lourdes environment peaceful and compatible with her personality, and she stayed there, graduating with honors in May of 1989. Throughout her educational experiences she pushed herself, often feeling inadequate and unprepared to meet the academic challenges. The completion of her Bachelor of Social Work degree demonstrated her capabilities and provided her with a number of employment opportunities. When she elected to work for the Family and Children's Services Bureau of Lucas County and was hired as a sexual abuse investigator, she was well aware of the potential danger but was determined to provide assistance needed by children and families in those situations. Her devotion to her work earned her recognition from the agency. She received a plaque, "In appreciation for dedication and unselfish service to the children of Lucas County," and it was an honor she cherished.

I believe every step she took along the way to Kalamazoo was part of a bigger plan. No one really knows how all these steps came together to fulfill her life's prophecy, but they surely did. Was there something I could have done to change the course of her life?

CHAPTER 18

Baking Christmas Cookies

In the mid 1980's, my sisters, mom and I decided it would be fun to get together to bake Christmas cookies. We'd pick a Saturday or Sunday usually a couple of weeks before the holiday for our group adventure in the kitchen and head off to one of our homes that had a kitchen large enough to accommodate all of us. Initially, everyone was to bring a recipe to share, and we would pool our baking resources to create our goodies. We all thought that we would be together for a few hours, enough time to bake maybe a half dozen recipes. But, of course, our desire to be efficient with our time never quite happened the way we intended, and we sometimes would spend six or seven hours on the cookies. And most often, we'd end up with eight or ten varieties, sometimes more. But, it didn't matter really; we had so much fun mixing and cutting and shaping the dough. Throughout the entire time we worked in the kitchen, we'd listen to Christmas music from different artists, different songs, and different styles. We'd sing along as we'd shuffle from one recipe to the next. Dani, Mom, Becky and Mary had a cute little dance routine they had put together to a John Denver holiday album. I don't know where that ever came from, but every time that tune would play, they'd stop what they were doing and dance together around the room. As the families with kids grew, we'd bring the nieces and nephews to share in our delight. My brothers were never invited; neither was my dad. This was another one of those things that my sisters and I, and often my mom, would devote our time and energy to. It was a wonderful Binkowski tradition that continues to this day.

Getting together was sometimes challenging, with work schedules, raising children, and distance between where we all lived. We met once at Sara's up in Adrian, Michigan, but usually we baked here in town. Our first gathering was in my mobile home, before Marsha and I bought Dani and George's house. Dani's oldest daughter, Caitlin, was probably just about three years old. Our location varied after that, but often it was on Bancroft. There were a few times that Sara was unable to come down to Toledo because of scheduling conflicts, and after Mary moved to California in 1990, she was obviously unable to join us a couple of weeks before Christmas, since she and Scott would make the flight in for the holiday.

In the few weeks before Christmas in 1992, we were all having trouble narrowing down the date for our holiday baking. We tried to plan it at least a couple of weeks before December 25th because everyone's schedule was usually pretty hectic in the days leading up to the holiday. But for some reason, probably by default, we picked the Sunday before Christmas. And, as luck would have it, Mary came into town the Saturday before. It was so nice being able to have her there, because she had missed the last couple of times we got together. Unfortunately, Sara couldn't make it down at all that year. So, Dani, Mom, Becky, Mary, Marsha and I came together at our house on Bancroft for our tradition. Becky had come in from Kalamazoo the night before and stayed at the house with us. Dani left the girls with George in hopes that we could move along through the afternoon, getting things done without lots of interruptions.

Over the years, we got smarter about making our always popular cut-outs. The dough requires about four hours in the refrigerator before baking. This particular time, Dani prepped the dough the day before, which cut down our prep time dramatically. What a brilliant idea! We should have thought of it years ago. In between our singing and rolling and cutting, we listened to Mary's latest stories from California. She worked for two women who owned a real estate management company, and from the sounds of it, they were quite successful. Mary was employed as their executive administrative assistant, and although she had little college background and minimal experience in that field, she worked hard and impressed her bosses enough to get promoted to that post. They liked Mary a lot and often treated her as a friend.

Mom was videotaping Mary who was describing a telephone conversation she had with Annette, one of the owners, when Becky started flashing a cute, colorful cut out cookie in front of the camera.

"Becky, what have you got there?" Mom asked as Becky sheepishly pulled the cookie away.

I think she realized she had interrupted Mary and started to back away when Mom caught her eye.

"It's an elf," she softly spoke. "It's for Hanna," she continued.

"Oh, that's so sweet," we all chimed in as she showed us the detailed piece. It was only a cookie, but she had taken so much time to make it so adorable that no one except for a child would ever want to eat it. It was the best dressed cut out I'd ever seen before or since that day.

I'm so thankful Mom brought her video camera, even though there were times she could drive us a little crazy with it. Mom liked to shoot just about every family gathering and every other thing that she ever attended, but she wasn't always prepared to start shooting on the spot. It often happened that something funny or something profound would pop out of someone's mouth and be the hit for those few seconds. But Mom would suddenly realize that she missed that Kodak moment, and we'd have to reenact the scene. We've been doing it for years, so Becky showing off her Hanna cookie was a cinch. I'm only sorry that Sara couldn't be there to throw in a laugh or two and share her baking specialty for the camera.

It was the last time Becky would come to one of our Christmas baking marathons. Although she had been at all the previous baking get togethers, this one stood out for me. I don't know if it was because Mom had the video camera or because Mary was able to be there or just because we had so much fun. Thank God Mom got the video footage she did, with Becky and that beautiful elf cookie!

Thoughts in Between number 18

I looked for you in the stars last night, and though the sky was full of sparkling lights, I did not see you. I stared out my window this morning hoping to find you there. In the gentle breeze, the trees swayed in the wind. I looked, but I could not find you there. I came into this room, once yours, and tried so hard to see you here, but my search was in vain. Some people say they can feel your presence when they walk in, but not me. I can't feel you here.

Now, saddened and alone, I look to myself this time. And, in the reflection of the light and my tears, I can see a glimpse of you smiling at me. And I realize something I've known all along: But through my eyes I could not see, in the stars or through the trees I cannot see you; but once I close my eyes and let my heart travel to the deepest part of me, there is where I find you, for always, you are inside of me.

CHAPTER 19

Christmas Day 1992

It was Christmas Day, 1992, and several of my family members were already at Birckhead when Marsha and I arrived. My mom and dad were both in the kitchen, busily preparing the feast that would be served later in the afternoon. They were engaged in the usual squabble over which one of them was in each other's way as they bustled about the room. Both of my folks are good cooks, and over the years they had taken turns dominating the preparations. This year was no exception. I entered the kitchen to express my holiday greetings and offer my assistance, which at this point in the day was usually rejected.

"Merry Christmas, Mom," I offered to my mother as I reached over to peck her on the cheek with a quick kiss.

"Merry Christmas, Lisa," she leaned towards me and smiled.

"Hey, Dad, Merry Christmas. Do you need any help?" I asked as I moved closer to kiss him on a rather sweaty left cheek.

"No, I don't think so. Not just yet anyway. Merry Christmas to you too," he answered back.

I took a quick look around the kitchen and knew if I stayed another minute I would just add to the chaos, and so I turned and sauntered in to the living room.

"Hey, Lis! Merry Christmas," came a greeting from across the room. It was Becky, sitting in my Dad's favorite chair, holding Hanna on her lap. Becky and Hanna had a special relationship, as many of my siblings and I do with the seven grandchildren in our family. As Hanna's godmother, Becky accepted the responsibility of caring for her in the event anything should ever happen to her parents. But more than the role of nurturing their faith, in our family, being a godparent was a big deal. We each savored the opportunity to spend extra time with our godchild, providing guidance, support, and an unspoken connection to our young charge.

"Hi Beck," I smiled as I leaned over to squeeze her and Hanna in one big hug.

"You look good! How was the trip?" I asked.

"It was fine; the roads were pretty clear," Becky replied.

Christmas at the Binkowski home has always been the most celebrated day of the year. With the exception of Jan, Rick's girlfriend, who was with her own family in southern Ohio, everyone came to Birckhead to spend Christmas together. Any celebrating with in-laws happened on Christmas Eve or the weekend following Christmas day. Christmas day, to our family, is sacred. We are meant to be together; it's as simple as that.

Over the years as our family grew, we attempted a variety of ways to curb the spending and the number of gifts under the tree. I know we all believe in the true meaning of Christmas without all of its commercialized fanfare and obligatory exchange of presents. We were raised to understand that Christmas in its purest form was about love and caring, peace and goodwill. But, of course, gift giving has always been a part of the holiday celebrating too. What kids raised Christian aren't anxious for a present under the tree? And so, this tradition has continued throughout the years. And as it has continued, every Binkowski has given a gift to every other Binkowski. When I walked into the living room to deposit my two giant trash bags filled with wrapped presents, the seven foot tree was already buried a third of the way up with gifts. And not everyone had yet arrived.

"Wow! That's unbelievable," I exclaimed, as I stared at the mountain of colorful packages.

Becky just laughed along with me. Dani and George were also in the room unloading large boxes of gifts, and we all stood there chuckling at the situation. It seems that every Christmas has been like this, with the exception of two years when we tried drawing names for a gift exchange. And although the sight of the pile surrounding the tree could be construed by a stranger as an obnoxious overkill of product consumption, I don't think any of the Binkowski's see it that way. As for me, I love the concept of giving gifts to people I love, and Christmas is the perfect time to do that.

None of us could ever afford anything lavish, and the quantity and value of each purchase is hardly relevant. It is the notion of giving that makes it so special. About two o'clock in the afternoon dinner was ready. At this point, all of the adults began assessing the seating situation. With so many bodies to seat and so many mouths to feed, we resorted to setting up two dining areas: one, of course, at the dining room table where twelve people could sit, and the other in the living room at a large folding table. We put seven chairs around it and added the piano bench to squeeze in a couple of the kids. After adding two more chairs to the dining room table, we were finally ready to eat.

As had been customary the past couple of years, Mom bought two large bottles of wine for toasting prior to eating. For the kids, she bought sparkling grape juice, but everyone called it fake wine. I think the kids felt like they were more connected to the toast if they had some "wine" too. Usually, Mom attempted to gain our attention by raising her glass and her voice. I'm not sure why I felt the need to do so, but I offered to make the toast this year, and Mom smiled at me as she nodded her approval. I stood up between the two seating areas and began my toast.

"Here's to each of us, family and friends. We are so very blessed to have such a wonderful family. No one really knows what the future will bring, and we should each be thankful every day that we have each other in our lives. I love you all. Merry Christmas!" I concluded.

We clanked each other's glasses around both tables as Mom stated, "That was really nice, Lisa. Thanks."

I don't know what it was about this day, but I felt very connected to my family and fortunate that we were all together.

Following dinner and clean up, the time for the gift exchange had finally arrived. The kids were so anxious, and understandably so. Who wouldn't be excited to tear through that mountain of packages? It seems that we each had our own special place around the living room for this occasion every year. Rick sat on the couch next to Joe, who had his daughter Alissa in front of him on the floor. Mary and Scott also sat on the couch. John sat directly in front of the couch with his daughter, Jessica, and Sara's family sat on the steps. Dad sat in his chair, closest to the tree, and Mom stood behind him with her video camera perched in her hands. At the opposite end of the room sat Dani, George, Caitlin and Cecelia. Next to them sat Becky and Rich, with Hanna nestled between the two of them. Marsha and I sat on the piano bench, as always.

Traditionally, Sara and I handed out the gifts, trying to get all the kids a present to open about the same time. Shrills of delight and surprise filled the room as my nieces and nephews tore through the wrappings.

I always try to give something of substance to my siblings, something from the heart. I want them to know they're special to me, and I always try to convey that in my gifts. This year was no exception.

"You guys always give such special presents. I didn't know what to buy; all I gave were these boring sweatshirts," Becky lamented from across the room. She addressed no one, but was really talking to everyone.

"I like my sweatshirt, Becky," I said.

Similar responses came from others in the room. Becky had bought everyone, including Mom and Dad, a Generra brand sweatshirt, in varying colors and designs. Mine was green, with tennis rackets across the front. I love tennis, and even though I wouldn't have picked this particular shirt for myself, I knew I would get good use out of it.

"Really, Becky; this is perfect for me. Thank you!" I walked over to give her a big hug, and as we embraced, we talked about how wonderful we both thought this Christmas day had been.

"This is the best Christmas ever," I said to her.

"Yeah," she answered. "No fights, no arguing, Mom and Dad didn't get mad at each other, and Dad even sat down for dinner with us. This was the best!" She replied.

Minor tiffs and disagreements scarred so many previous holiday gatherings, and sadly, too often, my father refrained from joining us at the dinner table. Instead, he stood in the kitchen nibbling directly from the pans. Sometimes, he and Mom would get so cranky with one another that he'd go upstairs and sit in his room until it was time to open gifts. But this year, he joined us at the table, enjoying the wonderful meal with his family. It was such a joy.

Sara overheard my conversation with Becky and added her thoughts.

"When the guys have their holiday toast, I think the girls should have one, too." Sara was referring to the annual Christmas day toast that my brothers, dad, and brothers-in-law shared several years ago. I really don't know what they drank or exactly what they toasted, since none of the females in the family were allowed to be in the kitchen for it, but I thought Sara had a great idea.

"Yeah! Let's get all the women together for our own toast!" I cried. The three of us gathered the other female adults and headed into the kitchen.

"What should we drink?" Becky asked.

"There's some wine left," Mom said, and so I grabbed the large bottle of Zinfandel from the porch and began filling our wine glasses. Dani, Sara, Mary, Mom, Marsha, Becky and I formed a half circle in the only open area of the kitchen and raised our glasses to the center.

"Here's to the women of the Binkowski family, the strongest women in the world who always stick together"! Becky offered as she held her glass high.

"Clink, clink," Mom chuckled as she held her glass to the middle of the half circle.

"No, it should be 'cheers'," Mary answered back. And so, we clicked our glasses together and cheered the beautiful day. It was fun, and we promised each other this would be the first of many holiday cheers from the Binkowski women.

Later, as the evening hours wore thin, Dani, Sara and their families began the task of gathering gifts, packing leftovers, and bundling up their tired children for the trek home. Although it was almost ten o'clock, I wasn't ready to leave.

"How about playing a game?" I asked the remaining siblings.

"That would be fun!" Becky said. "What should we play?"

We kicked around a couple of ideas before settling on the game of Taboo. It was one of the many games that Santa Claus had given to the

Binky kids over the years. Taboo is a game where there are two teams of players, and the object is to get your team to guess a word without using forbidden words. A player gives clues but can't say three or four words that are listed on the taboo card. On one of Becky's turns, she was doing her best to get a correct response but her descriptive terms were confusing. She was trying to get her team to say "Tom Seaver," a well known baseball player of the 1970's.

"He stands on the mound of the dirt!" She blurted out. "He throws that pigskin," she added.

I couldn't help but laugh at her attempt, and I was on her team. I think everyone in the room knew that a baseball pitcher works off the mound, but a football is made of pigskin. She was confusing the two sports, and the buzzer sounded before anyone could figure out what she was trying to describe. It was pretty funny.

"It's okay, Becky," Mary piped in. "You did good!" She added, trying to soften our teasing over the matter.

It was well after midnight when we finished up the game and all headed to our own homes. This was truly a wonderful day, and I couldn't remember enjoying a Christmas day from start to finish like I did this one. It was precious.

Thoughts in Between number 19

I honor your spirit, I cherish the memories, and I savor the life I was fortunate enough to share with you.

When you were alive, I cared for you, fed you, sang to you, played with you. I laughed, talked, and cried with you.

How I wish I had more time with you.

We did so much together, but it wasn't really enough.

Now I think of you, I cry for you, I pray to you, and I ache for you.

The thought of you is my greatest inspiration and yet, my deepest pain.

I love you, Becky. It never ends.

CHAPTER 20

Ski Trips Up North

For several years, Marsha and I took an annual trip to northern Michigan to cross country ski at a beautiful place called Sylvan Resort. It was nestled just a few miles from Gaylord, Michigan, where a nationally known golf course was converted into a ski Mecca for downhill and cross country ski enthusiasts. We always went on the long weekend with a Monday holiday for Martin Luther King's birthday, since the drive was almost four hours one way.

In January of 1992, Marsha and I invited Becky to journey with us, along with Marsha's friend Connie. Becky was living in Kalamazoo, Michigan, at the time, and met us about halfway in Ashley, Michigan, at George's parents' home. They let her leave her car parked in the drive, and after a short visit with them, we were on our way. The Gaylord area of Michigan is hilly with abundant pine forests, and in the heart of winter, the snow blanketing the landscape adds a wonderful touch of serenity to the view. Our evening arrival at the resort prevented us from venturing out into the woods for skiing, but after unpacking and fixing a quick bite to eat, we knew where our first point of interest would be: the outdoor hot tub.

There's nothing quite like the rush of dropping a towel just inside the hall and then scurrying outdoors about thirty feet to a bubbling whirlpool and stepping down into steamy hot water. It seemed a little crazy, but once submerged in the pool, the heat and swirling waters were a perfect way to finish the evening. We stayed out for forty to fifty minutes, occasionally reaching out of the water for a quick sip of our favorite brew and often giggling at the icy froth that formed on our heads from the falling snow as it melted above the heat and then refroze from the cold air. Every twenty minutes one of us would have to jump out and reset the timer to keep the jets in motion, and often Becky volunteered to brave the cold and ice to keep the rest of us happy. She was the youngest; it seemed only fitting.

Early the next morning we fixed our breakfast of bagels and cream cheese and then ventured out to the trails. It was Becky's first time cross country skiing, and she rented a pair of skis and the necessary gear for the weekend from the lodge at the resort. Surprisingly to me, she had a knack for staying upright on the skis and moved about the snow with relative ease.

The trails at Sylvan varied in their level of difficulty, and although none of us had much experience at skiing, we skipped the beginner trails and headed off to the ones venturing through the woods and up and down hilly trails. In the wooded areas, the paths are marked by red bumpers attached to trees to protect errant skiers, with most of these bumpers on downward slopes. I remember Becky laughing at first at the bumpers, but on her first journey down one of the treacherous routes, it quickly became apparent why those guards were necessary. We all took our turns at spills, especially in the woody areas, and fortunately, none of us had to actually use the bumpers to keep us and the trees from becoming one.

On our second venture out that day, we selected a different path to follow. We stopped at one of the posted trail guides, made a couple of mental notes on how to proceed through the trees and headed out. Becky was well in front, seemingly off in her own world as she glided along.

But she missed our predetermined turn off and continued on a previously taken route. The three of us stopped at the curve and called out to her to turn around, but she obviously didn't hear and kept trekking forward. As we positioned ourselves out away from the curve so we could catch her eye should she turn to look for us, I pulled out my camera and snapped a picture of her. She was quite far from us, and the picture of her gliding along at the base of a large hill captured a moment that I'll always remember.

To me, it was postcard perfect in showcasing a get away from it all experience: becoming one with nature in a beautiful, serene environment. Seconds later, Becky turned around and realized she was out there alone. We yelled across the pond and the open field, which seemed to be at least two football field lengths, to get her attention. Suddenly she saw us, quickly reversed her direction and almost frantically headed our way. When she eventually reached us, we all just laughed at how oblivious she was to her solitary travels.

The following year, in January of 1993, we made our plans to head up north to Sylvan for another long weekend of skiing and fun. This time, three other friends joined us for the adventure. As in the past year, we met Becky in Ashley, Michigan, where she dropped off her car and climbed in with Marsha and me.

Kindl, Robin, Marnie and Connie continued on in the other vehicle. About halfway there, I asked Becky if she wanted to drive. Late in the fall I had bought a new sports utility vehicle, a Mazda Navajo, and she was anxious for the chance to drive it. Becky got behind the wheel; I put in an Indigo Girls compact disc, and off we went. A short while later we encountered some heavy snow, with visibility barely above zero at times. I was a nervous wreck, and yet, I offered to take over driving because I was sure Becky was as nervous as I was, especially in a new car, in someone else's *new* car. She gleefully responded that she was fine and was okay, as long as I was okay with her driving my Navajo. I was amazed at her level of calm in such a difficult situation, and I let her continue.

The snowing and blowing eventually tapered off, and as the tension level in the car tapered as well, we simultaneously started singing along with the Indigo Girls' tunes. Each of us chimed in to a variety of the songs on the tape *Rites of Passage*, from the rocking refrain of "Joking" to the haunting words of "Ghost." But as we sang along with the lines of "Love Will Come to You," Becky suddenly had a revelation.

"I get it! I never knew what it meant, but now I get it!" She cried out, almost in shock about her discovery. "My words are paper tigers; no match for the predator of pain inside her," she repeated them as she listened. "They're just *paper* tigers . . . they seem strong on the outside, but they're kind of weak inside," she continued. She was so thrilled with herself at that moment, like she uncovered a deep secret that had been buried for years.

It made me think of a t-shirt she had bought the previous summer. I had a catalog from a company called "Northern Sun," whose specialty was liberal themed clothing, posters, buttons and the like. I showed it to Becky and she ordered a t-shirt that stated: "Listen to women for a change." When she read that statement, she found it to be incredibly profound. It wasn't just about listening to women; it was about hearing them in an effort to make change.

"Listen to women . . . for a *change*; get it? For a *change*," she said, over and over. "It's about letting women change the world . . . that's so cool," she commented, and simply smiled at the thought. I just smiled myself, knowing full well what the shirt was all about.

We finally reached our destination, and as we pulled into the parking lot, we met up with the car full of our friends. On this trip we reserved two rooms, with Becky, Marsha, Connie and me in one, and the other three in the other. Of course we followed our typical routine; fixing dinner in the room, hanging out in the outdoor hot tub at night, and two trips out to the trails on Saturday.

This year Sylvan Resort offered a new feature: tubing down the big hills behind the conference and lodging center. For five bucks we could rent oversized inner tubes to ride down the hills, and we were all eager to try this new ride. The only problem was walking up the hills once the ride was over. The tubes weren't heavy, but it was a long climb upward. The first several trips down, we raced each other and waged bets on who would finish farthest down the hill. Becky, Marnie and I took honors in the competitions, but we all had fun. After a while, the long haul up the hill exhausted everyone, and we spent the last ten minutes of our rental resting on our tubes at the top. That last run down would be the end of our physical activity for the day. Even Becky was winded from the cold and the climbing, and she seemed to be in better shape than the rest of us.

Later that evening, as we prepared dinner, we listened to music on the tape deck I had brought along. Becky asked if it was okay to put in one of her favorite artists. As I nodded with approval, she pulled out the Harry Connick Jr. tape she had recently purchased. If you are familiar with his music at all, you'll know that he models his style after Frank Sinatra Jr., with his classic, jazzy song selection and his suave, big swing music voice. I personally don't care for his musical style at all; Becky, on the other hand, loved it. She jumped up on the bed and started swaying and dancing to the song playing. She giggled at herself, knowing full well that her goofy antics would get a laugh from everyone else. She pretended to dance with a partner who swayed her back and forth, ending the song with a graceful dip of the shoulder and then a soft landing on the bed. It was funny to watch, and I couldn't help but reflect to myself: here's this twenty-five year old kid delighting in the music of Harry Connick Jr. It was strange to me, but then again, Becky had quite the eclectic taste in music. She liked funk to dance to, John Denver to sing along with, Amy Grant to appreciate a spiritual sense in songs, and Polish songs as a testament of her connection to her heritage. When she lived with me on Bancroft, I often played Pachelbel's Canon in D major, my favorite classical piece. Many times Becky listened to my album of variations on Canon in D when she studied, and it became her favorite too. She appreciated just about every kind of music, and I found it encouraging from someone so relatively young.

On the trip home, we talked about Mom's upcoming birthday on February 2nd. Becky was supposed to work that weekend, so I wasn't sure when I would see her again. As we bid our goodbyes in Ashley, she promised she would see what she could do to get out of work on the last weekend in January, but she didn't have much hope for getting it switched. As I watched her drive away, I remember thinking how proud I was of her and how much fun it was to spend time with her. I had lots of friends, but Becky was one of my best. It was rewarding to get to know her so well and to really love and respect the woman she was becoming. I hope I never forget that moment.

THOUGHTS IN BETWEEN NUMBER 20: LETTER TO BECKY #4

September 27, 1993

Dear Becky,

I've loved you as a sister and as a friend. But now, I must learn to love you as a memory, as a hero, as a saint. It's kind of hard to do when I remember so well changing your diapers and rocking you to sleep; helping you with homework and smiling as you blew out the candles on your 16th birthday cake. It's hard when I think about baking Christmas cookies with you and dancing with you in the living room to our favorite tunes. It's hard to imagine a saint from so long ago celebrating birthdays, baking cookies, or kicking up her heels to a song. I guess you'll just have to be a new kind of saint, and I'll just have to learn to love you as one. I'm guessing it won't be too hard to do.

CHAPTER 21

Mom's Birthday

It was Sunday, January 31, 1993, and my dad had prepared a special dinner for Mom's birthday. Her actual birth date is February 2nd, but because that date fell on a Tuesday this year, he made a big Sunday dinner so that everyone could celebrate it with her. Everyone but Becky and Mary, of course, would be there. I had spoken with her on Friday night, and as much as she wanted to head our way, it was her weekend for coverage at the apartment complex.

Much to our surprise and delight, just before dinner was ever set on the table, Becky and Richard walked in.

"I can't believe it! I thought you had to work!" I cried out joyfully.

"I was supposed to, but I asked someone to cover for me for a few hours. I didn't want to miss Mom's birthday dinner! I haven't been home since Christmas," Becky responded with the excitement of a little girl.

"Do they know you are here in Toledo?" I asked, knowing full well that one of the requirements of her position was to be available every other weekend in case any questions or problems arose at the complex.

"No, they don't know I'm out of town. Hopefully, nothing happens for them to find out!" She replied mischievously.

We were all happy to see her there. Our family gatherings, although always large and crowded, felt best when every member of the family could be there. And it was just like Becky to pull off a surprise like that, counting on a little bit of luck and good friends back in Kalamazoo to help keep things quiet until she returned. As Dad was scooping out the vegetables and potatoes into large bowls, Becky made a startling announcement. She and Richard were engaged! Just the night before, he asked her to marry him, and she said yes! They set a date of October 2, just about eight months away. As everyone took turns congratulating them both, I pulled Becky aside to talk to her privately.

"Are you sure you want to marry Richard? I know you love him and he's a good guy, but is this really what you want?" I asked earnestly. I knew that they had had their share of problems over the past year or so, especially when Becky went to Boston to work at a summer youth camp in Massachusetts called Hull House. It was there she met a guy that she spent a lot of time with, and whom she grew quite fond of during her stay that summer. She found that relationship so refreshing, and she kept in touch with him after she left the camp. Was she sure she wanted to spend the rest of her life with Richard?

"I've thought about everything else, and I know he's the one I want to be the father of my children," Becky explained.

"I know we've had our problems, but I think we can work through anything," she continued. I could tell by the look in her eyes that she had no reservations about this decision, and in fact, she was glowing with happiness. Her face was simply radiant, and I hugged her tightly as I whispered how happy I was for her.

"He's so lucky, Becky," I told her. "You'll make a beautiful bride," I said admiringly. She squeezed me tightly and smiled as she told me that she wanted me to play the music for her ceremony. She wanted me to be in the wedding too, but she was certain she wanted me to perform the music. She had it all figured out. Her first request was the song, "Ave Maria," a traditional, tender song that emanated reverence, solemnity and love. I pictured the song playing in the background of a candle lighting ceremony, and I knew it would be perfect for her.

She asked each of her sisters to be in the wedding, and each one of us beamed with pride. I don't think any of us could believe that Becky, our little sister, was actually getting married. Shortly after Becky and Richard made their announcement, my brother Rick said he had something to say. Not to outdo Becky, but he and his girlfriend, Jan, had decided to get married this year too! They had no immediate plans except for the date, which was August 7th of this year. Wow! It was kind of shocking to hear Becky and Rich announce their upcoming nuptials, and when Rick declared his and Jan's engagement, you can only imagine the excitement in the house. It was an incredible afternoon.

To celebrate this amazing day, Mom pulled out a couple of bottles, one of champagne and the other a chardonnay, to toast the two couples. As we passed around glasses to fill, Dad stepped into the dining room with a large goblet of shrimp cocktail. Instead of raising a glass of the champagne to toast, he proudly held up the goblet, grinning from ear to ear. We all raised our glasses high, saluting the two happy couples. We marveled at the coincidence of each couple making their announcement at the same time, and we all bubbled over with joy. It was an amazing day, and I looked around the room at my family, full of so much joy and good fortune.

Thoughts in Between number 21

I knew Becky her whole life. She was my baby sister and one of my dearest friends. I was very blessed to be able to be so close to her throughout her life. And I always knew that she was special to me, to my family and to her friends, but I never really knew how special she was to life itself until recently. The concern, the tenderness, and the love that has been pouring in is overwhelming and so very touching. I know now that we were all lucky to have her for as long as we did. She was larger than life, a messenger of God. She came to us to spread God's love, and she did it oh so well.

CHAPTER 22

February 3rd

The morning of February 3, 1993, was snowy and cold. It was a typical winter day in northwest Ohio. I had just come from a Directors' meeting with our Vice President and gone into my office to settle into the day's activities. Centered on my desk was a note that read, "EMERGENCY." All that was written was "Call home." I dialed Marsha's work number and before she could utter a word I asked what was wrong. She explained that she hadn't called, and I realized it meant a call from my parents' home.

Promising to call her back with any information, I hung up quickly and anxiously called the house in Birckhead. Joey answered the phone in a terse, shaking voice.

"Joey, what's wrong," I pleaded. I could tell he was crying as he replied.

"Becky's dead!" He started sobbing. As I gasped for air, I couldn't believe what I just heard.

"How?" I asked. "What happened?" I trembled with fear and disbelief as I tersely asked,

"How do you know?" I begged for answers. He told me that Richard's father, Albert, had called earlier that morning and told my Dad that Becky was in a serious car accident. Before long the phone rang again and Joe picked it up. He could tell by the tone of Albert's voice what happened.

"It was a car accident," Joe explained through his sobs. Becky was apparently on her way to work when it happened.

"I'll be right there," I told him and quickly called Marsha back at work. I could barely speak when she answered the phone. I told her what happened, and she said she'd leave work immediately to pick me up to take me to Birckhead. When I hung up the phone, I started screaming, helplessly and uncontrollably. I couldn't believe what I had just heard. My assistant Michael hurried towards me asking what was wrong. As I explained, I slumped in his arms, sobbing profusely. I'm sure he didn't know what to do, and I know now as I think about it that the news was devastating to him, too. The word quickly spread around campus and other colleagues came rushing into the Activity Center to see if there was anything they could do, if there was some way to help. But nothing could alleviate the pain or lessen the shock of what had happened, and I knew at that instant that none of us would ever be the same.

Joe and Steve still lived in Birckhead with my folks, and I'm so thankful that they were there to be with my parents when the news first came. I don't know what my mom and dad would have done without them there. Dad was home when the call came in, but Mom had been at church, getting her throat blessed for the feast of St. Blaize, the patron saint of throats. I was told that when she walked in the house and my brothers told her about Becky, she fell to the kitchen floor, ripping her cross off the chain around her neck. I wondered too, how could this God that Becky so loved let this happen to her? We were all in a state of shock as we embraced one another in desperation, sobbing, and wailing helplessly.

One by one, my other siblings arrived at the house. Rick and John came in shortly after I did; George had picked up Dani from her job, and Sara headed down from Adrian. Mary was working to get the next flight out of the Orange County Airport and would soon be on her way. Something completely unimaginable had happened, and none of us knew what to do. We were aching and crying inconsolably when the phone rang. I reached over and picked it up to answer.

"Who is this?" A voice asked on the other end. "This is Lisa," I said.

"Lisa, this is Albert, Richard's father. Someone needs to come here, to Kalamazoo," he urged.

"Can you bring your parents?" he asked.

"Why?" I asked. "Today?" I was puzzled by his urgency for someone in the family to get to Kalamazoo as soon as possible. But I could hear the urgency in his voice, and so I agreed.

"Yeah, I can bring them," I replied.

"There's something suspicious about the accident. Your parents need to be here," he stated.

"Okay," We'll be there as fast as we can," I offered.

"Good! How soon can you leave?" he asked, demanding an answer.

"Soon, I think. We can leave within a half an hour, ok?" I was puzzled by his insistence, but I was so dazed I really couldn't think straight. Marsha offered to drive, and shortly thereafter, the four of us headed to Kalamazoo, two and a half hours away. Marsha drove my Navajo with my father in the front seat, while Mom and I sat in the back.

As we sat in silence on that long journey, a hundred thoughts crossed my mind. What was so suspicious? Where was Becky going? How did it happen? Was she in a lot of pain? Was she by herself? Was she alone when she died? My head was spinning with all these miserable questions. I looked over to my mom, watching her cry softly as she stared out the window. I put my arm around her shoulders in an effort to comfort her, but she seemed to pull away from me as I tried to hold her. Suddenly, I thought about how close Mom and Becky were and how they enjoyed doing so many things together. Mom not only lost her daughter, she lost her baby. She lost the child who had so much promise, so much hope for her future. I couldn't bear my own pain, and at that moment I realized that her pain was far greater, most immeasurable, deeper than I could imagine. It was impossible to fathom. I started crying again, wishing that it was me who had died, feeling guilty for still being alive. Why not anybody other than Becky? Is that what Mom was feeling? I don't know, but I realized if there was ever a way to change what had happened, I would have put me in Becky's place. My parents were given the worst thing that could ever happen to a parent: having a child die before them. And worse yet, it was their youngest, their sweetest, their recently engaged child, their baby. I wished that it could have been me.

After all, I was thirty-nine years old, had achieved a lot of goals in my life, and so far had lived life well. But I had disappointed my folks with my lifestyle, and I wasn't as close to either of them as Becky was. And, simply put, I wasn't Becky. When an experience like this is thrust into your face, you come to some quick conclusions. I was so sorry that it wasn't me instead. If I could have done one thing for them that could mean more than anything else in their lives, it would have been that. That was the longest two and a half hours of my life, and there was nothing I could do to change that feeling at the time.

When we finally arrived at their home on the western outskirts of Kalamazoo, Albert and his wife Robbie were there waiting at the door. They came outside, and as we climbed the porch steps, my Dad asked about the accident. Without hesitation, Albert's eyes widened as he shouted out.

"There was no accident; Becky was murdered!" Mom fell to the ground; I thought she had passed out. What was this horrific reality we just heard?

"What do you mean, she was murdered?" My father asked in disbelief.

"Why, the man that killed her was one of her clients!" He continued as Marsha and I helped Mom back to her feet. I don't think anybody's footing was very stable as Albert continued his story. Apparently, Becky was attacked by one of the residents in her apartment complex. Albert then told us the police would be there shortly to offer more information about Becky's death.

We went into the house where the rest of Rich's family had gathered. I could hardly breathe as we stumbled inside into the kitchen. It wasn't devastating enough that Becky was dead. Now we hear that someone actually took her life. What kind of nightmare were we experiencing? A few moments later, the doorbell rang. It was the police. Officer Szekely shook Albert's hand as he ushered him inside. He expressed his sympathy as he introduced himself to each of us. We sat in the living room as he unraveled the real story of Becky's death. According to reports, Becky had climbed into her little Dodge Colt to head to a staff meeting that she was about to be late for. As she began backing out of the parking lot, her client, David Stappenbeck, knocked on her driver's side window. He needed a ride; could she give him one down to the corner where he could catch a bus? Of course, Becky readily agreed and motioned him to get in the passenger side. Within three blocks, he pulled out an eight inch blade butcher knife from an inside pocket of his coat and began attacking her. She tried to defend herself, but when he plunged the blade into her throat, he severed the major artery in her neck.

As Becky lost control of the vehicle, it slammed into a telephone pole on the right side of the road, and then lurched forward into two parked cars. A couple of men from an electronics office across the road heard the crash and ran over to see what happened. We later learned that when they approached the car, they found David humped over Becky, yelling. "Call an ambulance," in a frantic tone. As one of the men raced back to the office to make the call, the other fellow looked into the car. Becky was partially wedged between the seats where David had hovered over her. Her awkward position was likely forced from the thrusts of his attack that pushed her between the seats. Before the man could do anything to help, David climbed out over Becky, jumped out of the car, and started running away.

The witnesses said that when they arrived, blood was gurgling from her neck, and pooling out from the other wounds on her face. He had stabbed her nine times. She never had a chance to survive.

David Stappenbeck was a resident at the complex when Becky began working there as a residential supervisor in August of 1992. She helped him to manage his money, care for his living space, and interact with housemates and neighbors. It was never Becky's job to provide transportation to him, but she sometimes did to help him out. Becky lived at the apartments so that she could be on hand when little things came up, like this simple request of a ride down to the bus stop.

Thoughts in Between number 22

I can't stand the sounds of ambulance sirens; every time I hear that sound, it takes me to that horrible morning and I cringe. I envision the ambulance rushing to get to her, darting in and out of traffic, with the people inside thinking they were on their way to save a life. I wonder if Becky heard the ambulance siren, getting louder and louder as it pulled up near her car. What happened when they put her on that gurney and sped away to the hospital? Did they know what he did to her? Did they do everything they possibly could to try to save her life? Every time I see an ambulance, I think about how someone, somewhere, is hoping and praying that the worst isn't about to happen.

CHAPTER 23

Bringing The News Back
To Birckhead

It was after nine o'clock at night when we finally pulled into the driveway back home in Birckhead. Mary had arrived from California earlier in the evening, and I offered her a pained greeting as I hugged her at the door. All of the family was now in Birckhead, sitting together, crying, helpless and devastated at the loss of our beloved Becky. I don't think anyone could be prepared for what we had to share with them, and so I began softly.

"You need to sit down," I pleaded, as tears streamed down my cheeks. The shocking reality of what happened to Becky would be impossible to soften, and I knew it just had to be said.

"It wasn't an accident that killed Becky. It was one of her clients in the apartment," I choked out. I felt as if I were spewing the most evil of words that had ever been spoken.

The gasps and screams and horrific expressions on the faces of my dear family members added volumes to the heartbreak I could barely endure. Marsha helped me to explain the story of David asking for a ride this morning, only to turn on her and attack her with his knife. I told them how her little Dodge Colt crashed into some parked cars, which led bystanders and initially the police into believing it was an accident. And I told them how the first person on the scene ran to her car to help, only to find David hovering over Becky as she lay bleeding profusely and gasping for air. When I described how David yelled for someone to call an ambulance and then quickly climbed out of the car and ran down the street, the looks on some of the faces changed. I could see the anger and the need for retaliation intensify. In between the tears and the anguish seeped an immediate sense of urgency to go find that son of a bitch who did this to our sister. I told them how David was in custody and that he wasn't going anywhere. As the person who took on the responsibility to travel to Kalamazoo and bring the truth back to Toledo, I knew I had to be honest, but I had to keep my sanity too. Still, I had the same gut wrenching feeling that I wanted to go find him and slash his throat just as he had done to Becky.

We were encrusted in an impossible situation, a horrific nightmare that would not quit. When the news of Becky's death was first shared, it was beyond anyone's comprehension that this would actually happen in our family. It was an unimaginable horror. But, when the truth of her murder came out, the degree of pain plummeted into immeasurable depth. The question kept being asked, why would anyone want to hurt Becky? One of my sisters asked if Becky had been sexually assaulted; had she been raped first? Was this the reason for the attack? But, I suppose in some strange sense of relief, Detective Szekely assured us that David never attempted to sexually harm her. His intentions were to simply kill her. So, I guess that was one less thing we had to figure out how to cope with, even though it was impossible to cope with anything at this point.

We all stayed at Birckhead into the early hours of the morning, talking about Becky, her visit this past Sunday and her dreams of the planned wedding. We spoke a lot about the discussion Marsha and I had with Richard, up in his room when we were in Kalamazoo earlier that day. Richard stressed over and over how Becky and he had watched a television program the night before about burials and cremation. Becky had insisted that she would want to be cremated, and that she did not want anyone to see her after she was dead. I also told them of another disturbing thing that Richard mentioned when I was up in his room just a few short hours ago. Richard gave an eerie account of a conversation they had had not long ago that jolted me nearly out of my skin.

Becky had told Richard that even though she felt perfectly safe at her job, she wanted him to know that if anything ever happened to her, the police should look for David. She had the sense that she would die a violent death, and even though he had done nothing to cause her any suspicion, she mentioned that David could be the one who might harm her. I said I was stunned because it reminded me of a conversation we had on the way up north just a few weeks before when we went skiing. It reminded me of us talking about death and how I thought I would live long just like our grammy, who was ninety-two years old. And then I told them how Becky had stated quite matter of factly that she thought she would die young and that she thought it would be at the hands of someone else. When I told this story, my brother-in-law Mark jumped in the conversation because he said that Becky had told him the same thing a while ago; that she would die violently. How did she know this? And what about the TV program about burials the night before? She made Richard promise that she would be cremated and that no one, not even him, could see her. Oh my God; this was all so bizarre! And, on top of that, we had learned that although Becky was stabbed several times, the one that killed her was the assault to her throat. And here it was, the feast of St. Blaize, the patron saint of throats. I'm sure I wasn't the only one whose head was swimming with this crazy mess of information. I was numb from the shock and in so much pain, I don't remember leaving Birckhead that night. The only thing I really knew is that somehow, I was still breathing and my precious Becky was dead.

Thoughts in Between number 23:
Letter to Becky #5

My Dear Becky,

Today marks twenty years since the day you were so tragically taken from us. February 3, 2013. Where did all the time go? It seems like only yesterday I saw you in Birckhead, smiling and laughing with your family. So many of my memories of you are still fresh in my mind. I close my eyes and I can see you talking in the hall about your upcoming wedding, beaming with joy. I can almost hear your giggle as you talked about sneaking away from work to spend the afternoon with us for Mom's birthday. I am so sad that all I have are memories; and even though twenty years have passed since I last saw you, my heart aches deeply and tears have welled in my eyes. I don't think the pain will ever find its way out of my heart.

We decided to honor you on this sad day of remembrance and prepared a gathering for anyone who would care to come. We invited family, friends, classmates, and people who never had the privilege of meeting you but knew of your story and your impact on those you left behind. We brought many of your possessions that we've treasured over all these years and displayed them for everyone to see. I was so touched as I watched our guests, one by one, study your letters, your pictures, and all the pieces of your memory that we shared today. They were moved by the thoughts of you once again, as we all were.

Becky, I am so certain that anyone who ever met you was profoundly touched by you, by your genuine kindness and by your beautiful spirit. No matter how much time passes by, regardless of how the years add up, you will never be forgotten. It is impossible to lose someone etched into the very core of one's soul; that's where you are.

I have loved you your entire life, and I will love you for the rest of mine. You are with me in every way, every day.

I love you Becky, more than you'll ever know.

Your big sister,

Lisa

CHAPTER 24

The Reality of Her Death

There are really no words fit to describe the days that followed the horrific news of Becky's death. I found myself in a kind of vegetative state, convinced that this nightmare was just that; it couldn't be true. I found myself stumbling around, unable to eat or sleep, crying intermittently when I would let myself think, sinking into deep despair. Somehow, I managed to keep breathing. As I look back, I don't know how any of us survived losing her in such an unfathomable manner.

We didn't have a perfect family life, but we had a GREAT family. Always close, always supportive, always there for dinners, birthdays, and trips to the lake. How could this family continue with one of our pieces missing? Nothing would ever be the same, and never would we feel "whole" at any get together ever again. How were we going to survive?

I truly think that the same love that so deeply moved Becky, moved us forward the days after her death. It seemed like we became more loyal and more protective, if that was possible, all fully aware that she was the first of us to die, and we had to do whatever was necessary to keep the rest of us alive. This experience was so incredibly overwhelming, I think we recognized there was no way we could deal with losing someone so close to us again, especially like that. Not that we had any control over her death, but we could control how we lived our lives from then on.

Joey talked about suicide so many times, it was frightening. He had struggled with his own insecurities since his early teenage years, and often his instability wreaked havoc on my mother's nerves. But Joey would never do anything to hurt his family. This is what I have to believe and always hope he believes, too. He continued to struggle along, although the pain in his face was raw and unnerving.

I look back on so many days when I myself thought about running out in front of heavy traffic just to try to escape my misery, but I couldn't do it. And I am sure that all of my siblings felt the same despair, the same hopelessness of going on without Becky in our lives. The pain was so often just too much to bear.

This new reality of Becky's death, not specifically her murder, but the simple truth of her dying was excruciating. No one ever expects someone so young, healthy, and happy to die. Knowing she was home just three days before, sharing the excitement of her engagement, glowing with joy made this truth seem all the more unreal. I begged to wake up from the horrific nightmare, but I knew nothing would change. She was gone and a million prayers said by the holiest of religious leaders could do absolutely nothing. This tremendous pain was here to stay.

Thoughts in Between number 24

In 1996 I was asked to speak at the Toledo Take Back the Night March and Rally, an event to raise awareness about violence against women. This event has been held across the country in many different communities for several years. This is what I shared with the participants:

She was spirited and she was spiritual; A feminist who was feminine;

An activist who was active;

A servant who served; her name is Rebecca.

These words are taken from a memorial plaque dedicated to Rebecca Ann Binkowski. She was born March 7, 1967. She died February 3, 1993. She was twenty-five years old, the youngest of nine children, three months away from graduating with her Master's degree in Social Work. She was engaged just four days before her death. She was giving, caring, compassionate, genuine and kind. She was devoted to her family and loyal to her friends. She was zealous in her work and generous with her time and energy to causes she believed in. She was a lover of humankind. She was murdered by a mentally ill client who had no apparent motive but found her to be an easy target. She was my youngest sister and one of my best friends.

Becky was the victim of a violent act because the man who killed her knew that he could. He knew her schedule, he knew she would travel alone that morning, and he knew she would give him a ride if he just asked. He had other caseworkers who met with him regularly, but he picked her as his victim. Why? Because he was mentally ill? Definitely! Because he knew her caring personality and knew that she would surely step into his trap, giving him a ride on that cold, snowy morning? Absolutely! Because he knew that he could overpower her with his large, six foot frame in that restrictive subcompact car? I'm sure of it!

Because she was a woman? Yes! Could he have pulled it off if he had attacked a male caseworker? Would he even have tried? I don't know, but I don't think so.

For myself, I have struggled most of the 991 days since she was killed. Although on paper my experiences and accomplishments have been many and memorable, I don't remember them well. Many I don't remember at all. My emotions are locked into February third, 1993, and quite often, I feel that I will never break the emotional grip that holds me there.

That's why, when I was asked to speak tonight, I said, "yes." As with countless other women, I know the effects of violence against another human being. And I know what it's like to suffer from the actions of a man who knew he could succeed against his female victim.

And so, I ask myself, What do I do? What can we do to stop feeling so damn helpless in the aftermath of such a horrid experience? We opened a store in my sister's honor. We're working on creating a community center dedicated to her. We have scholarships in her name. We've written stories, poems, songs; built memory gardens; made t-shirts. And these are all wonderful tributes to her life in her memory, and I wouldn't take back any of these things. I'll continue to honor her in different ways for the rest of my life. But what can I do? What can we do to keep something like this from ever happening again?

We gather like this to demonstrate our anger and frustration. We gather to say we refuse to let male domination rule our lives and frighten our streets. We gather to send a message that says we defy aggressive behavior as an acceptable part of life. And we persist in our efforts to remind the members of our society that every life is precious and deserves to be treated with kindness and respect, no matter what. Life is hard enough. We don't need to make it harder for each other. What we need to do is convince those who don't believe or understand or agree with the simple concept of valuing the life of another human being, every other human being. Until kindness and respect replace aggression and the hostility, we must continue to gather like this, and we must be seen, and we must be heard.

This is why I am here. This is what Becky's death challenges me to do. This is what she would do if only she could be here to do it herself.

CHAPTER 25

The Next Two Days

The next morning, word spread quickly about Becky's murder. Family, friends, coworkers, and friends from church called or came to Birckhead to offer support and condolences. Trays and plates and bowls of food filled our dining room table from end to end. Everyone tried so hard to be helpful in this helpless situation. Someone mentioned that arrangements would need to be made to bring her body back to Toledo and that some kind of service should be planned. Everything was such a blur that day. I found myself sitting at the funeral home with my mom and dad, but I can't recall who else was there. Surely other siblings were there with us, but I was so numb the details escaped me. I did know that her body would be brought back to us the next day, Friday, and that she would be cremated, just as she desired.

On Friday morning, there on the front page of the newspaper was Becky's picture and a lengthy article about her murder. Over and over I read that article, dazed by the truth of it all. Relatives continued to come to the house in Birckhead, bringing food, desperately trying to ease our pain in the midst of their own tears.

We received a call from the funeral home that Becky's body had arrived. Several of us went with Mom and Dad to finalize plans for the gathering later that evening and the service that would be held on Saturday morning at St. Hedwig Church.

As we rode the short distance from Birckhead to the church, we talked about how horrible it was to not have the chance to say goodbye to Becky. But we had agreed to honor her wishes, that no one would see her. Even in the small parlor where we met with the fellow who helped us with the planning, we talked about wanting to see her to say goodbye.

Finally, we agreed, most reluctantly, that it was probably best not to see her in the condition she was in. As we talked, Dad left the room. I thought that perhaps he was going to talk about payment, but when he returned several minutes later, his face was ashen and his gait unsteady. He sat down and started crying. Then, he softly spoke.

"I had to see for myself that it was really her," he sputtered.

Oh my God, I thought to myself. He went to see her? He looked over to my mom, and she was obviously upset. But he assured her it was better that she didn't see Becky. At first, I was angry that he snuck away to see Becky, that he got to say goodbye. That he maybe got to touch her one last time. I was jealous for a moment and then I realized it was a crazy thing to be jealous about. I knew then that he would always have that image of her burned in his memory. One more scar from this nightmare was his and his alone. I think he was right to shield Mom from that experience, as well as the rest of us. Even so, being that close to her and not seeing her wreaked havoc on my emotions for a long, long time.

Thoughts in Between number 25

A friend of Becky's shared this with me in the spring after her death:

Ode to Rebecca

Life is not just time between birth and death; It's so much more.

Life is a plum; fresh, growing, mature, choice, even wrinkled.

Life is the moon; new, beaming, full, setting, eclipsed always phases.

Life is stories bearing witness and luminescing the nature of one's own character, little anecdotes woven into a single unique fabric.

Rebecca taught me this.

Telling the story is what gives us meaning.

This is how we come to know Him.

You heard about the tree falling in the forest; Has a life been lived if nobody tells her story?

Harold Systma May, 1993

CHAPTER 26

Visits And Funerals

On Friday night we headed to the funeral home in the Polish village to welcome family and friends. It's a strange thing to prepare for, not knowing who will meet us there to pay their respects, to offer comfort, and to grieve for this unexplainable loss. Soon after my family's arrival, people started pouring in the doors: friends of Becky's, friends of mine and my siblings, aunts, uncles, cousins, neighbors, old schoolmates, members of the church. The air was filled with weeping and wailing from every direction. Every time I closed my eyes and hoped that this was all a horrible nightmare, the sounds of crying and sniffling brought me back to my reality. She was really gone.

Soon every room of the funeral home was packed with wall to wall people, sharing hugs, telling Becky stories, and sharing more hugs. I was grateful that so many of my friends and coworkers came for me and my family, but I found myself gravitating to my sisters and brothers throughout the evening. They're the only ones who could understand me without my having to say a word; and every time I stood with friends, I found myself speechless. The helplessness was overwhelming, and I was numb to the bone by the end of the night.

On Saturday, February 6, we had arranged a funeral mass for Becky at St. Hedwig's. We all met at Birckhead before heading to the church, and piled into cars together to share the ride there. Even though it was just a few short blocks, it seemed to take forever to get there. Once we got there, I wished it had taken longer because I was not ready to experience a funeral for my baby sister. Nonetheless, it was another challenge to face in this awful nightmare of life. When we arrived, the church was full, with standing room only. There must have been five hundred people in that church. How did they all know Becky, I wondered. I was blown away by the size of the crowd, and I was grateful that so many people were there to share such a sad time with us. A couple rows in the front were saved for us and we slowly made our way there.

We had agreed that we would wear the sweatshirts that Becky gave us for Christmas. The gift that she thought was just some silly shirts had now become our mantel of tribute to her. It never occurred to me what people must have thought when the entire family marched into the church, pulled off our winter coats, and stood there in an array of colors instead of traditional black. It was for Becky and nothing else mattered.

The priest conducted a typical Catholic mass but instead of a traditional church song during the communion, the soloist sang "Wind Beneath My Wings" from the movie Beaches. It was a perfect song for Becky with these lyrics: "Did you ever know that you're my hero? You're everything I would like to be . . . I can fly higher than an eagle, you are the wind beneath my wings," and so on. I started thinking about how Becky, so young and so innocent, was such a remarkable young woman; how she had such insight and purity. I thought about how she called me her hero when we were at the lake last summer. And now, it was clear to me; she was my hero. I didn't know it when she was alive, but I most certainly knew it from that moment forward.

Near the end of the service, the priest invited anyone in the congregation to share a few words about Becky, if they so desired. I slowly stood up and went to the front, up the few steps into the pulpit. I tried not to cry, but the tears accompanied my words.

"I have known and loved Becky every second of her life; she was one of my best friends. Even though there were thirteen years difference in our ages, we were connected deeply," I shared.

"I can tell by the number of people in this church that she has touched more lives than I would have imagined. I believe her life has been a gift to each and every one of us, and for that, I can say that I am so blessed to have been so close to her, to have shared life with her these past twenty-five years. I can remember when she was very young and I spent a lot of time taking care of her because our mom had started working nights. Becky called me "mom," and although it bothered my mother, it was so special to me. It's one of those things I will never forget. I don't know what I'm going to do without her," I finished.

I slowly walked back to my seat as Dani made her way to speak. She called Becky an angel, and I know she was right about that. One by one, people in the crowd took their turn to talk about this gentle soul, their inspirational friend, the charming young woman who made such a difference in their life. People had written poems, recited verses from the Bible, told stories about their time with Becky. Every story was precious. And everyone was hurting so deeply. I could hear it in their words, and see it on their faces; Becky meant so much to so many people.

As I listened, I found myself getting a little possessive. She was MY sister, she was our sister. All these people who wanted to say something about her; I was thankful about it and yet, I started feeling a bit overwhelmed by their connection with her. What the hell was wrong with me? I appreciated the stories, but I found myself thinking: okay, I see that you are sad and grieving, but your grief is not like mine; she is MY sister. I had no empathy for anyone else except my family and Richard. I was empty and exhausted. By the time the last person went up to speak, this part of the service had lasted more than two hours.

The next day we traveled to Kalamazoo for a church service there. Since Becky had made this city her home the past two years, it was the right thing to do. We joined Richard's family at their church and made our way to the front two rows. Although the church was much smaller than St. Hedwig's, it accommodated a fairly large number of people. Again, just like the day before, throngs of people filled the church, row after row. Soon, people were lined up against the walls on both sides, filling it beyond capacity.

The minister spoke kindly of Becky, as if he had known her for a long time. At one point in the service a vocalist approached the altar to share a song. As soon as the pianist began playing, I felt my spirit crumbling. As soon as the first few words, "Ave Maria," left her lips, I began trembling, fighting the unbearable urge to start bawling. "Oh dear God," I thought to myself, "not this song. Not the song I was supposed to sing for her wedding!" I couldn't stand it; I couldn't bear it. Thank God, it finally ended.

Shortly after that, the minister invited people in the church to share a few words about their memories with Becky. One of Richard's brothers went to the front and spoke on his behalf because he couldn't bring himself to speak. Other friends of Becky's made their way to the front, to share their sorrow over her death, their stories, their poems, their love for her. I realized at that moment that I had to say something, but it needed to be different from yesterday.

"I am Becky's oldest sister, and I love her, and I miss her, and I don't know what I'm going to do without her. I never wanted her to move to Kalamazoo, and I had always hoped at some point she would move back home to Toledo. But I can see by the number of people here today, that it was right for her to move here. She needed to be here so that she could touch your lives, too. I wanted her for myself, because that's what a protective, older sister does, I guess. But I know now that she was meant to share her life with all of you, too. I know, too, that I've been so lucky to call her mine. I see by this outpouring of sadness and love that Becky belonged to you, too. I'm glad that you love her so much and got to know her so well," I said sadly.

Several other folks in the church came to the front to talk about Becky. It blew my mind again. These tributes went on for over an hour. I was amazed by how much Becky meant to all these people, most of them strangers to me, and yet, their stories told the depth of Becky's impact on their lives, over and over again.

When the service had ended, we all went outside to release some balloons in honor of Becky. It was windy and cold, and one of the balloons got stuck in some branches of a huge tree about a hundred yards away. Just as the crowd began to lament about the balloon, a gust of wind seemed to magically untwist the ribbon tied to it, and it swiftly blew away from the tree and off into the distance. We all knew that somewhere up in heaven Becky was watching, and she appreciated the balloons and wasn't going to let a few old trees interfere with the experience. She had the last say that day, that's for sure.

THOUGHTS IN BETWEEN NUMBER 25

At the church service in Toledo, my youngest brother, Joey, made a few comments that showed his anger and despair. Joey knew that he wanted to say something more positive about Becky at the service in Kalamazoo, and in the car on the way there, he came up with this poem. Nervous and in pain from his grief, he read it to the standing room only crowd. It was beautiful.

Becky the Rising Sun

Once upon a time there was a boy

Who viewed the world as a broken toy

He couldn't see beyond his frown

Always saw the sun as going down

Then came a girl who was full of life

Saw the world in a different light

She took the boy by the hand

With her he traveled across the land

She showed him things he'd never seen

Took him places more beautiful than dreams

She wanted him so much to understand

That there's love within every woman and man

She told him that she had struggled, too

It's not always easy doing what you have to do

But with faith in God and family and friends

You will make it until the end
She left the boy knowing that he understood
To go out into the world looking for the good
He misses her so much because she's gone
But he knows she's there with each rising sun.
I love you, Becky. Thanks for making me see the light.

Joey

CHAPTER 27

Living In The Aftermath
Of Her Death

In the days and weeks that followed Becky's murder, life around us all went back to normal, and friends and colleagues seemed to ease back into their routines. I held nothing against anyone, but there was nothing normal for me to go back to. Life as I knew it had ended, and to pretend otherwise was impossible for me. I don't know if it was fortune or misfortune, but my siblings who have children had to attempt to settle into normalcy for the sake of the kids. I don't really know how they did it, because I was constantly consumed with severe depression and anger. I worked, but at the end of the day I didn't remember what tasks I had completed, where I had gone or what needed to be done the next day. I was hollow inside except for the intense pain.

The only ones who really understood me were the people who shared my loss, my family. And we all coped differently with losing Becky. This death gripped us in every imaginable way, and whatever means any of us had to survive, we had to use them. For me, I had to talk about Becky, I had to cry about her, and I had to think about her, all the time. I'm quite certain that this constant image of her in my mind and outpouring from my lips were attempts to keep her alive, to not let go of her. Maybe if I kept her constantly with me, maybe she wasn't really gone. If I didn't let go, maybe this harsh reality would fade. I played this cruel trick on myself day after day, week after week. I just couldn't bear the truth.

David, Becky's killer, had been jailed since the day of her death. His mental illness was the key factor in how the legal system would handle him, although I didn't care if he was mentally ill or not. He killed my sister, for no obvious reason. If the legal system didn't bring him to justice, I was afraid someone in my family would, myself included. I never doubted he knew what he was doing when he attacked her, and I prayed for his suffering in the same way he caused Becky to suffer. This ongoing train of thought caused me great internal conflict and wreaked havoc on my deep regard for humanity.

The family gathered often, usually on Sundays. At one point when Mary was in town, we held a meeting to try to sort out what would lay ahead. Richard's brother Wally was an attorney, and he offered to help us settle Becky's estate. He recommended that someone from the family be designated to work with him on that. Because I didn't have children and was one of the oldest, I offered to work with Wally. I absolutely did not want my mom or dad to have to deal with that, and I believed that I could handle the difficult work that would go along with it. Everyone agreed, and I made my first of several trips to Kalamazoo to discuss Becky's estate shortly after that meeting.

Wally was kind and thorough and did his best to make the task as easy as possible. Going through her bank statements and bills was tolerable, but viewing and holding a copy of her death certificate brought me to tears. I often cried most of the way home on those trips, but I knew if I wasn't crying in my car, I would likely be somewhere else crying over her death. I just couldn't stop myself, no matter where I was or what I was doing. I still couldn't believe she was dead.

THOUGHTS IN BETWEEN NUMBER 27

A friend in Kalamazoo read this at the memorial service there:

REBECCA ANN BINKOWSKI

Although death has stolen, death has not taken.

For in living, Becky left so much; she can never be gone.

Is it not memories that keep a person in absence alive?

Did Becky ever hug you, comfort you, or give you a smile;
read you a story, or make you laugh?

In doing these things, Becky was saying,

"Here—I'm with you, let me touch you."

She had so much love, and she gave so much love;

It touched so many.

Her Christ-like example will live forever.

As you struggle on, don't leave Becky behind;

take her with you, not as a sorrow, but as she had lived;

full of life, love, and eternal happiness.

Author unknown

CHAPTER 28

The Case of David Stappenbeck

David was truly a paranoid schizophrenic, aggressive and anti-social. On March 16, 1993, in Kalamazoo district court, David was ruled incompetent to stand trial. The ruling was made not because he did not understand the charges against him, but because doctors did not believe he could assist his attorney in his defense. The judge said that there would be a status review in sixty days, and in the meantime, he would remain committed to the mental hospital where he would receive treatment. This ruling gave us all increased anxiety, anger and frustration with the judicial system. When David admitted to slashing Becky's throat, he stated that he knew right from wrong. He made up an excuse about the cuts to his own hands, and he hid the evidence in a dumpster. I couldn't understand how all of these blatant facts couldn't stand on their own merit. Sure he was ill, but he murdered someone, and he knew it. The irony of all of this is that because he was unstable at the times they tested him for his competency, he was unfit to stand trial for a murder he already acknowledged. He admitted guilt; why should there be a trial anyway? The only question at hand, as far as I was concerned, was whether or not his punishment would fit what he did to Becky. Michigan-unfortunately, in my opinion-doesn't put anyone to death, regardless of the crime. I had never been a proponent of the death penalty prior to his actions, but all I could think of during this time was how unfair it was that his life wouldn't end as Becky's had. There was nothing fair about any of this, that's for sure.

Over the following months, several facts emerged about David's history with mental illness and criminal behavior. He was diagnosed with schizophrenia when he was a teenager. Multiple times in the mid

1980's, he was charged with a number of misdemeanors and placed in detention centers. In 1987 he was charged with setting his mother's home on fire and found incompetent to stand trial for that charge. He was committed to the psychiatric hospital for 90 days for the arson. He had been in and out of treatment facilities, as well as jail for breaking and entering charges in 1990. In August of 1990, David was sentenced to prison for the felony breaking and entering and larceny charges, but served just a little over a year because of a suicide attempt. He was placed on parole and ordered to get treatment and take medication as prescribed for his mental illness. In July of 1992, he was hospitalized in the Kalamazoo Regional Psychiatric Hospital for entering the bedroom of another resident in the home, wielding a knife. He was discharged after a short stay and ordered to remain in the county mental health program for 90 days. Three weeks before David killed Becky, he admitted himself to that facility because of suicidal thoughts. He left the hospital on his own, following a two week stay, on January 16, Kalamazoo mental health officials maintained they had no indication that David would become violent in the Arlington Apartments or that he was dangerous. They also downplayed the knife incident because it was only a butter knife. On February 3, 1993, he attacked Becky in her car, mercilessly stabbing her to her death.

With this extensive history of crime and mental illness, how was David Stappenbeck placed in the Arlington Apartments, free to come and go as he pleased? My dad, who wept daily since Becky was killed, questioned the county's mental health system decision to place him there. If it took doctors from the forensic psychiatric center a little more than a few weeks to determine he was incompetent to stand trial, how could anyone ignore his history and put him in the apartments? Where was the logic in this?

Richard told us that David used to sit in his and Becky's apartment to listen to music. In a fit of anger, he smashed his own CD player, and so they invited him into their place. Richard was adamant that Becky wasn't aware of his criminal past, that he had a felony record, or that he threatened a fellow resident with a knife. She never knew he set his mother's house on fire either. But, she did have that strange feeling about David, just as she told Richard and his parents shortly before her death. Was it a premonition? How did she know she would die an early death? How did she know to look for David? How did all of the case managers and doctors and the other experts not have any sense that he could be so dangerous when Becky had a sense after being around him just a short time? All the tests and observations and confinement over the past several years didn't give them any suspicion? It just boggled my mind and made me so angry I could barely breathe when I thought about it.

Thoughts in Between number 28

February third is a day I will remember for the rest of my life. It's also a day I wish I could forget. I wish I could go back to that morning and creep into the mind of David Stappenbeck. What was he thinking? Why was he thinking the things he thought that morning? I'll likely never know what possessed him to deliver the fatal attack on my Becky. No, instead the things I'll know are these:

—I will spend the rest of my life without her, and I'll miss her constantly.

—I'll never hear her laugh, see the glow in her eyes when she smiles, or watch her clap her hands in excitement when something brings her joy.

—I'll never see her dance or bask in the summer sun or bake me her favorite breakfast sweets.

—I'll never be able to hear her voice on the phone, or get a letter from her telling me that she loves me, or hold her hand when we sit to pray before meals.

—I'll never get to feel her arms around me in a tight, loving embrace; and I'll never get to see her in the assortment of clothes she always wore and looked so beautiful in, and I'll never be able to see her sleeping peacefully on my couch.

David Stappenbeck, you took a part of me when you took my Becky away. Now I can only look at her pictures, wear her sweaters or her shoes, listen to her favorite songs, and re-read the old letters and notes. It's not enough, and it will never be enough. And they say you will plead

NOT GUILTY??!!

CHAPTER 29

Honors And Tributes

The impact of Becky's death was like a strong ocean tide. It affected not only her family and friends, but social work students, the schools she attended, the field of social work itself. Three scholarships were established in her name: at Central Catholic High School in Toledo, Lourdes College in Sylvania, and at Western Michigan University. At Lourdes and WMU, the scholarships are given to students pursuing a social work degree.

In April of 1993, social work students and human service workers at WMU officially changed their human service organization to the Rebecca Ann Binkowski chapter of the Bertha Capan Reynolds Society. This society, founded and named in 1986 for this well known social worker, works toward social justice for all people, especially children. One of Becky's WMU professors, Don Cooney, came up with the idea to change the name to honor Becky because he believed that Becky embodied the ideals of the organization and said that she was a great role model for members to live up to. Don had taught Becky over the past several semesters and had gotten to know her quite well through her academic efforts and her work in the community. It was a special tribute from those who knew and admired her work ethic.

On April 24, 1993, Becky was awarded her graduate degree from Western Michigan posthumously. We all made the trip to Kalamazoo to be there for her, even though we knew it would be extremely difficult. The University decided to present Becky's degree separately from the regular ceremony. Robert Wertkin, an associate professor in the School of Social Work, thought that it was important to honor Becky and to award the degree because she was so close to completion. Following the conferring of degrees to the other Master's degree graduates, we were invited to a small room behind the stage. There, the president of the University, Diether H. Haenicke, presented her degree to Mom and Dad while the rest of us sat nearby. Becky's education was so important to her, and she worked really hard at it. She finished her academic career with a 3.75 grade point average.

In the fall of 1993, the Kalamazoo County Mental Health Board adopted nine proposed reforms to help protect social workers from potentially violent clients such as David Stappenbeck. The reforms include extensive criminal background checks on clients, improved record keeping, and a mandate that social workers have access to these records. The Human Services Director for the county said that these reforms were broad based and did not imply that there were policy lapses that led to Becky's death. He actually defended David's placement at the Arlington Apartments, calling the decision a sound one, based on complete information about his clinical and criminal history. Wally, Richard's brother, attended the hearings on the committee's recommendations and publicly stated that Becky would have been more cautious had she had more information about him. With all of these reforms being implemented, it seemed quite obvious to me that there were flaws in their policies and procedures. In addition, the Family and Children's Services Director suggested that Becky knew David's background as well. I found it hard to believe that a well educated individual, who took great precautions in other aspects of her everyday life would be totally neglectful of her well-being around someone with a violent and volatile history. Unfortunately, how much Becky or any other staff persons with the agency knew about David would never be disclosed because of a state law protecting the privacy of mental health clients.

The president of the Local Alliance for the Mentally Ill at the time disagreed with the position the county officials took. She claimed that if Becky were aware of David's background, she would have been more cautious, and to suggest that she did know, was blaming Becky for her death. I was angry and disgusted with the notion that the County and Family and Children's Services felt they did everything right in placing David in Becky's care. They were so busy defending themselves that they forgot about the excruciating pain of everyone's loss. Still, to know that they approved changes to protect social workers like Becky was important and necessary.

On April 5, 1998, the National Association of Social Workers celebrated their 100th Year of Professional Social Work in Washington DC. A part of this celebration included remembering fallen heroes- social workers who died in the line of duty-and children whose lives had been saved by social workers. Becky, along with eight other individuals, was recognized for her ultimate sacrifice. The ceremony was held on the Mall, at the West Side of the Capital Reflecting Pool, with music, readings, and the laying of floral wreaths for each social worker. Mom and I traveled to DC to attend the event and to be there to honor Becky. Many members from the National Office of the NASW attended, as well as local dignitaries, family members of other fallen heroes, and other guests. Although the mention of her name was brief, knowing that Becky was recognized by a national organization in Washington, DC was incredibly profound. Even as I cried when I heard her name spoken and read her name in the program, I was extremely proud of her. She truly was an amazing woman. I couldn't stop thinking about how much more she could have done if she were only given the opportunity.

Thoughts in Between number 29

At the memorial service we held for Becky on the second anniversary of her death, one of her friends from the Lutheran Church stepped forward and spoke to everyone there. She cited passages from the poem, *Funeral Blues* by W.H. Auden to help convey her thoughts and feelings:

> ". . . . She was my North, my South, my East and West;
>   my working week and my Sunday rest . . . ."

I met Rebecca when she was hired to be the Youth Director at my church. We hit it off instantly and soon surpassed the youth/youth director relationship and became friends. It didn't take long for our friendship to become very strong and for her to be someone I treasured.

So, as far as friends go, she was my north, my south, my east and my west. She was always there with an open ear, a strong shoulder, and one of the brightest smiles I've ever seen. She embodied everything I wanted to be-intelligent, articulate, beautiful, passionate, and her integrity and faith were unsurpassed. She shone so brightly that I saw many things in a new light. Many things held a greater meaning for me and even things I dislike looked a little better.

> ". . . .The stars are not wanted now; put out everyone;
>   Pack up the moon and dismantle the sun. . . ."

Two years ago, that light was shut off. In anger, I put out the stars, packed up the moon and dismantled the sun. Fortunately for me, they were never really gone. They still shone as brightly as they did for the twenty-five years Rebecca smiled on them. It took a while, but I see them now and smile and think, Wow, Becky, you look beautiful today. Because now, she's part of them. She's part of everything. To see her, all I have to do is look outside at the children playing in the streets, or at the trees blowing in the wind. And when I need to talk to her, I know I still can. She still helps me with my problems and decisions and I know she'll always be there at every milestone I pass, cheering me on.

Becky was the Youth Minister at that church for about two years, working ten to fifteen hours a week. I was amazed at the profound impact she had on this teenager, and yet, I knew that this was just one of countless examples of her influence on the lives she touched. Wow, she truly was a gift.

CHAPTER 30

Tallulah's

In the months that followed Becky's murder, I was determined to honor her in whatever way I could. Marsha and I had toyed around with the idea of opening a feminist gift store at some point, because the Toledo area had nothing like it around. We had gone to NOW (National Organization of Women) meetings to network with other feminists in the area, and the summer before Becky's death, went to the National Women's Music Festival to check out artists and vendors who could potentially supply us with merchandise to carry in the store. Initially, Marsha would run the store, since I had a good position with the college and had a better income to support us. When Becky died, it all changed.

One of the many restless nights in the spring of 1993, we were lying in bed talking about our dream of opening a store. I kept thinking about Becky, how she affected so many people in her short life, and how she made such a difference in their lives and in her community. I was frustrated with my job at Owens and complained to Marsha that I needed to make a difference too. It was comfortable for me to stay at the college, earn my living doing the same things day after day, but I didn't feel as if I was doing anything really important. She told me that maybe I should leave Owens, and we should open up that store. We just looked at each other for a few minutes, and we both knew right then and there that we would open our store. We made a list of what we needed to do to make that happen. We would need a place, a significant loan to purchase merchandise, and a plan of how to run a successful business. We decided that Marsha would keep her job, and I would run the store. It was exciting and yet terrifying; I had never had any business experience, and we would be foregoing my salary. Even with these obstacles, it felt perfectly right. Before we turned off the lights, I leaned over to Marsha and told her, "I know what we should call the store," and before I could spit it out, she said back to me at the same time: "Tallulah's!" It was meant to be.

Over the next couple of months, we assembled a business plan, approached our bank for a loan, and secured a location about five minutes from our home. We were fortunate to get approval for our loan, signed the lease, and got all the necessary documentation and permits to establish a business. We contacted several businesses about merchandise, hit resale places to get display racks and shelving, and renovated the space to make it inviting and peaceful. On one venture into a local flower shop, we noticed that they had several fountains. We both lamented that it would be so cool to have a fountain running in the store but knew that it was likely out of our budget. Even so, I wandered into the back of the shop to look at a fountain of a woman holding a vase that was about four feet tall. I thought to myself that it would be really cool to have a fountain of a female in a corner of the store, and I shook my head as I reached for the price tag, knowing it would be expensive. One hundred fifty dollars was the first thing I saw, but then I looked closer at the description of the fountain, and it took my breath away. The name of the woman holding the vase was Rebecca! I yelled for Marsha, and once she saw the tag, she nodded in swift agreement that we just had to have this fountain. We would figure out how to afford this! It was meant to be ours.

We opened Tallulah's on July 1st of 1993. The preparation of starting a new business was challenging but at the same time, therapeutic. Every day was filled with a long list of tasks to complete, but it never diminished our enthusiasm. I was devoted to honoring Becky, and this store seemed like a natural fit for that. Besides Marsha and me working on the renovations, many of my family members got involved with it, and it was very fulfilling to have them be a part of this endeavor. My brother John and my sister Dani designed our logo, and my dad painted the sign that would be placed at the street in front of the store. Mom, Mary, Steve and Joe helped often, painting, setting up display racks, and organizing merchandise. Several friends helped too, and it was truly a testimony to Becky's spirit that we all worked together harmoniously and efficiently. When we opened that first day, it was scary, not knowing if anyone would walk through our door, but I knew that it was the right thing to do. I felt I was at the exact place I needed to be, that everything happened as it should, and I actually found a sense of peace in opening Tallulah's. Honoring Becky did that for me, and I had a new sense of purpose.

Over the next five years, people came from all over Northwest Ohio and Southeast Michigan to visit Tallulah's. Six days a week, I managed the store, and I told her life story every chance I got. There was an aura of serenity in that space, and I knew Becky was there with me. It didn't take away the sadness or the anger or the sense of loss, but I did my best to keep her memory alive in a positive way. I do believe that her story, the spirit of Tallulah's, and the connections we made with the countless women and men and children who came into the store made a difference. Even in her absence, Becky continued to touch lives.

Thoughts in Between number 30:
Letter to Becky #6

March, 1993

Dear Becky,

I think I'm gonna make it because I believe in the power of your spirit within me. I loved being your big sister, but even more than that, I loved being your friend. Living with you as an adult helped me to see what a beautiful woman you'd become, and it made me very proud. When you told me that you always looked up to me that night at the campfire at the lake, I was overcome. I didn't realize I had such an impact on shaping your life. I felt sad because I also realized I didn't have a role model myself, someone I wanted to be like. But, you know, now I realize that in your leaving, you can fill that void for me. You, who loved life to the fullest and gave to the world whatever it would take from you, even your life, you are my role model, my hero. I hope that I can find the courage, the strength, and the determination to get past the sorrow and the anger to follow your spirit and give to life what I can. Thank you, Beck, for your love, your care, and your friendship. Your life has been a gift, and I'll cherish every memory of you deep in my heart. I'll see you one day, and I'll be waiting for that hug from you I didn't get when you left. I love you Becky, and you will be with me every minute of my life.

Lisa

PS: Thought you'd like to know this, you little feminist; Marsha and I decided on the name of the store this morning—Tallulah's. Hope it's okay with you.

More Thoughts in Between number 30

On the second anniversary of Becky's death, I shared these thoughts with those who attended the memorial service at Tallulah's.

Rebecca Binkowski died too early to leave a legacy that the world might experience. But to those who knew her and shared in her life, she left a lasting impression as a beautiful spirit, a caring soul, and a woman with a heart filled with love for mankind that is rare and precious as life itself.

Becky; daughter, sister, aunt, fiancé, friend, co-worker, classmate; she embraced all of these relationships in her life. She always knew how to make those around her feel special. And, she did it without trying. She did it just by being herself. She had an infectious smile that could light up a room and gave the kind of hugs that could dissolve any kind of bad feeling.

It's hard to believe that Becky's been gone for two years. It barely seems like two weeks, let alone two years. The memories I have of her are strong and clear, from the most beautiful, touching moments sitting around the campfire with her, to the horrible details surrounding her death.

I cling to all of these memories; the laughter and the songs, the pain and the sorrow, knowing that every experience with her has made a difference in my life. From her youth, I learned the essentials of caring for a trusting and innocent child, characteristics that stayed with her until her death. And in her dying, she showed me the best way to honor and love humankind: with decency, respect, and compassion. I only hope that I will grow to be more like her as time passes by.

Becky's life has touched countless individuals, many of those we will never have the privilege of knowing. But there have been a tremendous number of women and men who have shared moments with her, and I've been fortunate to hear those stories. I'm lucky to work here at Tallulah's, this sort of shrine for her, and meet people Becky befriended. So many times people are reluctant to speak up at our first encounter, afraid that bringing up her name in conversation will only make me feel worse. Trust me; I will never feel any worse than I have.

Instead, I say, share your stories. Speak her name. In doing so, you keep her memory alive. You keep her spirit burning strong in our hearts. Tell me; tell the world, what a wonderful human being she was. And tell us all what an inspiration her life story has been. In doing this, we can continue to change lives and make a difference in her name.

CHAPTER 31

Finally, A Trial

David had been deemed incompetent to stand trial no less than four times since March of 1993. Finally, he was cleared and given a trial date of May 10, 1994. Fifteen months had passed since he delivered those fatal blows to Becky, since our world was turned upside down, since he destroyed our family life as we knew it. Sure, we all went on with our days and weeks as best as we could, in whatever way we could make it through. Living without Becky was already so difficult, and now, we were about to experience another horrible episode in this life without her.

Richard's parents had invited us to stay at their home on the outskirts of Kalamazoo as often as we needed to throughout the trial, and that was a welcome relief. Being two and a half hours from Toledo would have been tough to drive every day, and we appreciated their hospitality immensely. And so, all of my siblings with the exception of Steve, who stayed behind to work, and my dad, whom we believed just could not handle the trial, headed to Kalamazoo.

Mary flew in from California, and along with Mom, Rick, Dani, Sara, John, Joe, Richard's family, and me, arrived early on Tuesday, May 10th, at the courthouse for the first day of proceedings. The first order of business was jury selection, which involved interviews with the pool of candidates summoned for the trial. We all sat in the courtroom, listening to both the prosecutor and the defense attorney as they asked a variety of questions about their knowledge of the case, along with their opinions about other related topics. Finally, a jury was chosen on Wednesday, and the trial was set to start on Thursday, May 12th.

Before the trial got underway, Kalamazoo County circuit Judge Richard Lamb announced to spectators that the first row of benches would be blocked off for security reasons. He was concerned that people were getting too close to David when he was being ushered in and out of the courtroom the first couple of days and that he needed to guarantee his safety. Imagine that; he had to make sure the murderer was safe! It seemed outrageous to me that this move insinuated one of us would harm him. Sure, we all thought about it, but to suggest it was an actual possibility, there in front of television cameras and reporters and law enforcement officers, was simply ludicrous and offensive. My mom and siblings and I sat in the second row, while Richard's family sat right behind us. This was our place each day we came to the courtroom, day after day, week after week.

When we arrived at the courtroom in the second week of the trial, Judge Lamb had imposed further restrictions on the visitors. Greeting us at the entrance to the courtroom were two sheriff deputies, one to inspect our belongings and the other to wave a metal detector around each of us. We were not permitted to bring in anything without it being scrutinized. Marsha had brought a bottle of water, and the deputy ordered her to take a sip. It was confusing at first, but then we realized perhaps they were suspicious we may be bringing acid or some other poison to throw at David. Every day they opened our purses and our bags, and waved the wand around us from head to toe, all for the safety of a killer. To make matters worse, Judge Lamb ordered that no pictures of Becky be on display in the courtroom so as not to influence the jury. That was outrageous, but I figured a way around that ridiculous order. I had t shirts imprinted with a photo of Becky on a beach, her arms outstretched to greet the sunrise. The image was small enough to make her unidentifiable, but we all knew it was Becky in the photo. She was with us in spite of that edict, and it brought a small measure of comfort for those of us who wore those shirts.

The first person to speak was the Assistant Prosecutor, Carrie Klein, presenting her opening argument. She said that although David Stappenbeck pleaded insanity, his behavior was very methodical and showed every element of first degree premeditated murder. She stated that he caused Becky's death, he planned it, and he knew enough to dispose of the knife he used. She would introduce mental health experts and other key witnesses who would prove David was not insane at the time he killed Becky.

We also heard from pathologist, Dr. Adonica Walker, who performed the autopsy on Becky. She told the courtroom how Becky had defensive wounds on her hands, showing she fought the person who stabbed her to death. Her palms and fingers were cut where she had grabbed the blade in her efforts to try to stop the attack. She described how Becky had bled to death, estimating that she lost more than three liters of blood-half of her body's blood supply-between the site of the attack and the hospital where she was taken.

The two men who raced to the accident scene from across the street gave their accounts of what happened. Charles Vandermeen and Timothy Keeney, who worked at Lamplighter Electrical Contractors, saw the car crash into a row of parked vehicles in the lot of a school across the street. They both described how the car windows were fogged and initially, they didn't see anyone inside. They turned from the car and headed to the school when they heard a faint cry. Mr. Vandermeen yanked the driver's door open and found David squatting in the front seat, yelling for an ambulance. Becky was wedged between the two front seats, pushed to the back of the car. As the two men worked to pull Becky's body from the car, David disappeared.

As soon as Kalamazoo Township police officers arrived on the scene, they knew this was not a simple car accident. There was little damage to the car, and yet Becky was covered with blood, and the inside of the car was full of blood. Richard, after coming upon his fiance's car, told the officers to look for David. In addition to questioning him, they searched the apartment complex and found a 13-inch knife in the trash dumpster and blood stained clothing stuffed in a pillowcase hidden under a porch behind David's apartment.

To hear the details of Becky's attack and death was indescribably painful for all of us. I could barely breathe listening to the vivid explanations of what happened to her that morning. It's a crazy, messed up thing to be obsessed with needing to know everything about what happened and then be paralyzed to the core by the information. And yet, that was me throughout the trial. I couldn't turn away from it while it was slowly killing me inside.

Over the next three weeks, we lived in Kalamazoo from Monday night through Thursday, hearing testimony after testimony. Detective Szekely testified that he interrogated David, just hours after Becky's murder. He said that David told him he killed Becky because he wanted to spend the rest of his life in prison. He initially told the detective that he was insane, but when pressed whether he knew right from wrong, he admitted that he did. He explained that he didn't want to live in society because he wasn't suitable. When asked how he got into Becky's car, he simply stated that when she walked out of her apartment, he asked her for a ride, which she gave him. He planned the attack about two hours before he got into her car and described how he hid the knife in his jacket pocket. He figured this would get him confined to prison for sure.

John, David's roommate at the time of the killing, also testified. He described how on his birthday, Becky sang a Polish birthday song for him, explaining afterwards that she hoped he lived one hundred years. He said that he never complained to anyone, but he did fear David. He said David often lost his temper for no reason, and so he locked his bedroom door at night. He stated that he was shocked David killed Becky because she went out of her way for him, most recently when he asked her to help him get more intense treatment.

Both David's Mother and sister testified that they feared him and would not be alone with him. His mother described how he set fire in her home, directly below her bedroom, and how on a trip to Minnesota, David had thrashed around the back seat of the car, leading her to believe he was about to throw himself out of the car. He later told his mom that he had a dream about her, that she was dead with a knife in her back. His sister talked about how intimidating his behavior had gotten during his teenage years. His sudden outbursts of temper and violence, his talking to the voices he said he heard in his head, and his erratic behavior scared both of them so much that they didn't want to be near him.

A number of psychiatrists and psychologists testified for both the prosecution and the defense. Dr. Philip Margolis, a forensic psychiatrist, explained that David's mental illness did not meet the state's definition of insanity. His mental illness had nothing to do with his anti-social behavior or his fits of anger that may have provoked his attack on Becky. Dr. Thomas Shazer, a clinical psychologist at the Center for Forensic Psychiatry in Ypsilanti, told the court that David was not insane when he assaulted Becky. His schizophrenia only sometimes impaired his thoughts, moods, and behavior. It did not mean that he was always psychotic, and by the evidence from police and eye witnesses, he was not psychotic at the time of the murder. Dr. Shazer said that it was clear David knew the penalty for his actions was prison and that he could appreciate the wrongfulness of his act. Because he left the crime scene, washed the blood off himself, and hid the clothes and the knife, and lied about how he cut his hand, he clearly had control over his actions. To find him legally insane, his attorney would have to prove that he was out of control, but Dr. Shazer's testimony provided strong proof that this was not the case.

Finally, on Thursday, June 2, all the testimonies and arguments had ended. William Schlee, David's defense attorney, blamed the mental health system for failing his client. He said it was only a matter of time before David would kill somebody. Carrie Klein delivered a powerful closing argument, recognizing Becky's life was cut off far too soon, with no rationale but the lack of regard for life by her killer. She said that his mental illness might be a way he tries to excuse his behavior, but he must bear the burden of the life and soul of Rebecca Binkowski for the rest of his life, however long that may be.

Following the closing statements, we headed across the street to the small tavern we had frequented throughout the past several months. We had no idea how long deliberations would take, although we were told the longer the jury deliberated, the more likely they were considering acquittal.

Less than two hours later, we were summoned to the courtroom. Nervously, we filed into the second row for the verdict. The jury foreman stood up and read the words as we held our breath: GUILTY but mentally ill! Under Michigan law, the sentence for first degree murder is life in prison without the possibility of parole. Because the jury found him mentally ill, David would receive special mental health services throughout his incarceration, but he would never be a free man for the rest of his life, and he would never have the opportunity to harm another innocent person again. We were overcome with emotion when the verdict was announced, each of us crying profusely.

So now what? The roller coaster ride of the trial was over. It brought some closure for sure, learning all the facts about her death, knowing that David would be behind bars, keeping him locked up forever. But Becky was dead, and I knew at that moment that this wasn't really over for me. Changes in the mental health system were imperative. We lost Becky because of flaws in the system, and I knew we needed to be advocates for change. It's all we could do for Becky, and I promised her right then that I would do all I could to not let her death be in vain.

About five years into David's incarceration, we learned that he had hung himself in his cell. Initially, I was glad that he was dead. But that sense of satisfaction soon dissipated. It didn't bring any relief to the pain of missing Becky. It only meant that the poor bastard finally did what he should have done before he attacked her in the first place. I wondered if Becky met him at the gates of hell. Knowing her, she probably bartered with St. Peter to send him to Limbo instead. And, I'm sure she forgave David for what he did to her. But that's something I will never do. I hope Becky forgives me for that.

Thoughts in Between number 31

On the first anniversary of Becky's death, her colleagues at Family and Children's Services held a fundraiser to create a memorial garden in her name. It was filled with beautiful perennials, shrubs and colorful annuals, all arranged around a rustic bench where visitors could sit and reflect. At the dedication ceremony, one of the staff members assembled a collection of thoughts and comments about their time with Becky. Here are a few of their words:

Rebecca Ann Binkowski was a beautiful person who could not be forgotten—not in life and not in death. Rebecca had an impact on the Kalamazoo community far greater than most people will ever have; that's because she strived to make a difference.

We loved and will remember many things about Rebecca. She was the essence of energy and light. She said several times that she wanted to be "the best social worker she could be."

Rebecca must have been well loved growing up in her large family because she really knew how to give of herself with compassion and patience. Those are skills that can't be taught—they are instinctive in the very best social workers. She renewed our spirits and energized those of us who have worked in the field for a very long time.

The day Rebecca died, the sun was shining in Kalamazoo. The sun also shone on Thursday and Friday, in the middle of what is usually a dark and dreary Michigan winter. We know why. It was heaven's tribute to Rebecca; a gentle farewell to her loving warmth, light and energy.

We stand beside you in honoring her. She was cherished by all of you and it showed in the way she lived her life. Her life was a celebration of your love for her. We will miss her deeply. We know how much she wanted to make a difference in life. We want you to know that she did.

CHAPTER 32

Life Goes On

A lot of time has passed since that trial ended in 1994, and a lot of things have changed. Life has gone on without Becky in it, although I don't believe there's been a day since her death that I haven't thought about her. I have spent a lot of time grieving for her, aching over her murder, and reeling in her absence. I've let her death consume so much of my life and so much of my energy. My obsession with her interfered with my work, with my relationships, with my well being. And still, I will not abandon her or the memory of her life. I can't help but remember the painful parts as well as the good times. I know that they say time heals the wounds and helps you get over sadness, but, I don't think I will ever be healed. I think that I have been broken and that is the way I will stay for the rest of my life.

Being with Becky changed me in many ways I never recognized until she died, but I think about it all the time now. Her sweet innocence, her lack of pretense, and her love of life gave me a new appreciation of living life to the fullest. Seize the day, I often think to myself. You never know when it might be your last. I know that in the past, I often had reservations about doing something different, about being bold and trying new things. Now, I think about Becky's path in life and how she ventured in so many different directions in her short years. She wasn't afraid to try new things, and if she was, she didn't show it. I think about her warmth and compassion for people regardless of their age, intelligence, wealth or culture. She embraced and valued everyone, even the one who took her life. I think about how she would handle all this attention brought to her after her death. I'm guessing she would be embarrassed, because she certainly didn't seek out the limelight. She just went about her business, taking care of people who needed her. It seems that she knew her purpose in life, and that's what she set out to do every day.

How did this young woman come to understand her purpose? After she died, a number of different people spoke to me about how they thought Becky was really an old soul, that she had lived many lives and had the experience of an old sage. They told stories of how she inspired them, taught them, and comforted them, with wisdom that was simply amazing for a person just twenty-five years old. And because she was a wise old soul, that's how she knew she would die young and violently; and that deep inside her, she was aware and she was okay with it. She knew her life's plan, her purpose.

I continue to be in awe of the way she touched so many people's lives, and I hope to make a difference in the world, just like she did. I've got a lot more life under my belt, and still, I aspire to be more like her even now.

Time keeps on flying by, and the world continues to change. In my little corner of it, life evolves as it should. But one thing will never change, and that is this: I was lucky enough to know Rebecca Binkowski, intimately and significantly. I was blessed the day she came into my life, and through her life and her death, my life is richer and more fulfilled. Because of her, I have seen great joys and great sorrows, and they help make me who I am today. I don't know how long I will inhabit this earth, but I hope and pray that in some ways I have made her proud. I hope that from whatever heavenly loft she has perched upon, she knows that I miss her and that I love her. And if I had a miracle in my pocket, I would bring her back just for a moment to see her beautiful smile, feel her tender embrace, and thank her for simply being her.

THOUGHTS AFTER NUMBER 32

4700 days

I can't believe it has been so long since you were stolen away.

You'd think after all this time it would get easier, but I can say, it truly is not.

I look at your pictures, and I see a beautiful soul, timeless life in my gaze.

I wonder if you'll recognize me, or do you even know me now?

Age takes its toll, and there are times I have worn thin inside.

I'm afraid I'll forget, and I'm afraid you'll forget me.

I know that love knows no boundaries, but still, time continues.

It takes energy and memory and desire, all the things I need to know you.

And it scares me to know the possibilities that lie ahead.

I miss you, and I need to miss you. It is part of the reason I am living.

In silence I see your face, as I bring you deep into my being.

Often I close my eyes to keep any distraction out of my view, only seeing you.

And always, yes always, there is accompanying pain.

There is no joy in your absence, only overwhelming sorrow that never seems to end.

And yet, I allow it, because I fear that if I don't feel that, I won't feel anything.

Being sad is a part of remembering you; it's much of remembering you.

This is my life, and my life without you.

It is what it is, until I can see you again.

THE END

www.ingramcontent.com/pod-product-compliance
Lightning Source LLC
Chambersburg PA
CBHW051527120626
46551CB00012B/1106